# Seeking the Heart
## of Teaching

*Adrian Palmer*
*MaryAnn Christison*

Ann Arbor

THE UNIVERSITY OF MICHIGAN PRESS

#154666458

10-25-07

Copyright © by the University of Michigan 2007
All rights reserved
Published in the United States of America
The University of Michigan Press
Manufactured in the United States of America

♾ Printed on acid-free paper

2010     2009     2008     2007          4        3        2        1

ISBN-13: 978-0-472-03226-6
ISBN-10: 0-472-03226-7

Dedicated to Earl W. Stevick

# PREFACE

## STRUCTURE OF THE BOOK

### Purpose

As the title of this book suggests, we believe there is a heart or a core to teaching. We also believe that if teaching as a career is to bring us happiness over the long term it is important for each one of us to find what is at the heart of teaching. *Seeking the Heart of Teaching* is a book about teacher development: the process of developing the internal and external resources to support your knowledge of subject matter and teaching strategies. It provides opportunities for structured reflection on professional and personal development and offers suggestions for how to implement change.

### Audience

If you are a teacher who loves to learn about yourself and wants to experience how learning more about yourself can improve student learning in your classrooms and help you become a more effective and efficient teacher, then *Seeking the Heart of Teaching* is for you. It is intended for both new and experienced teachers because no matter how long you have been teaching and no matter how old you are, there is always more to learn about teaching. Teachers who are newer to their careers may find that this book presents a number of issues to explore and pathways to consider that will be important in achieving their long-term goals as teachers. Mid-career and master teachers will find this book gives them a different perspective on the pathways they have followed and on the many different paths still open to them.

### Presentation

This book is primarily written in the genre employed in professional publications, such as journal articles and books in teacher development series, but we have kept the tone friendly and informal. The main body of the text is intended for all readers. In addition, we provide footnotes and endnotes. Footnotes are reserved for short notes and references. Endnotes are more speculative in nature and explore certain topics in greater detail. Neither the footnotes nor the endnotes need to be read to make sense of and follow the main body of the text.

We use the conventions of conceptual frameworks and figures to explain and support ideas in this book. While we find that these figures help us in thinking through and understanding the concepts, we also recognize that this may not be true for everyone. We all learn in different ways. We hope the figures and conceptual frameworks are helpful to you because the essential information is chunked and presented in a visual summary that can make it easier to remember the information presented. If you find that the figures are not useful memory aids, we also believe that it is possible to focus on the prose and understand the ideas presented.

### Evidence

We offer an extensive array of references from a variety of disciplines and genres to support the hypotheses in this book. In some cases, the references are included to provide empirical support for claims or arguments. In many other cases, they are included to indicate that the hypotheses and ideas we are writing about are not unique to us and that other disciplines have come to similar conclusions from different bodies of research and a wide range of experiences. Many of the quotes, which are taken from individuals both within and outside of academia, are designed to serve the same purpose—i.e., to enable us to make a connection between teachers' professional and personal lives, which may vary widely.

## TEACHER CHANGE

*Seeking the Heart of Teaching* can be viewed as a book about teacher change although the types of changes explored in this book take time to implement. It is unlikely that dramatic changes will result simply from reading this book or any other book. Nevertheless, we know from our own experiences that reading has often planted the seeds of change in us and has supported the changes that occurred later in our lives. Ultimately, you must find your own ways of engaging with the concepts and suggested strategies in this book for implementing change over extended periods of time.

# ACKNOWLEDGMENTS

We would like to thank the many students in our classes with whom we have interacted over the past three decades. We have learned what we needed to learn from you and from our many interactions. At various times we have wondered if there was not an easier way to pursue our own development, a way in which our students did not have to experience the trials of our own development as teachers. Thank you for putting up with our rather steep learning curves at times and for helping us to learn about teaching.

We would also like to thank the many gifted teachers we have as friends (a list far too lengthy and extending too far into the past to recall in its entirety or to cite accurately). You have helped us discover and learn more about the internal world of teaching and helped us strengthen our experience of the relationship between the internal and external worlds. We are forever in your debt.

Finally, we would like to thank Kelly Sippell, Executive Editor at the University of Michigan Press, who had confidence in our original ideas and encouraged us to write the book. We thank you, Kelly, for your patience and support and for not giving up on us. We thank you for your good humor.

# CONTENTS

"I do not believe that teaching is a role we play in front of students or that to be a good teacher we must develop a special persona. I do not think we should strive to be someone different in the classroom or faculty meeting from the person we are in real life. The same values and strategies should guide us in all spheres of our lives. Our students and colleagues should not be surprised when they encounter us in an unfamiliar setting—the behavior they observe there should be consistent with their impression of us. In fact, I believe that the most important teaching we do is that which is often called modeling—the unconscious messages we send merely by acting the way we act."

Mark A. Clarke
*A Place to Stand: Essays for Educators in Troubled Times* (2003, p. 4)

# Chapter 1

# An Introduction

## MAKING CONNECTIONS

Teaching has afforded us livelihoods that have been personally rewarding in terms of the interactions we have had with our students and colleagues and in terms of the opportunities we have had to learn and grow as individuals. In fact, we believe that teaching is the best profession and work there is! Like many teachers, however, we have had some bumpy rides on occasion, and at times the road has been difficult. Nevertheless, we persevered and have been rewarded beyond our wildest dreams.

We don't believe our experience as teachers to be unique because all teachers struggle from time to time, especially in the beginning and especially in response to change. However, we have often wondered why we have stayed with teaching as a profession while other colleagues—some we have known over the years whom we thought to be inspirational and talented teachers—decided to leave teaching to pursue other careers altogether.

The answer to the question as to why some teachers stay with teaching while others do not is one that troubles citizens, elected officials, institutions, and governments. Teacher attrition has become a major concern in many countries and for many institutions from public schools to universities in both public and private sectors. In the United States alone, at least 2 million new teachers will be needed in the next decade. That's about 200,000 new teachers a year.* In addition, recruiting and retaining teachers has reached a crisis in many other counties with more than 50 percent of new teachers today choosing to leave the profession within five years.** We recognize that the reasons teachers decide to leave teaching are complex and varied: Some have to do with problems inherent in the educational system, such as low salaries, crowded classrooms, or lack of public support, while others clearly reside within individuals. If the problems associated with teaching are not resolved over time, the stress associated with these problems will take its toll on performance and on the sense of well-being that teaching can afford us as individuals. It seems that in order to remain in teaching over the long haul and experience the ways that teaching can be both personally and professionally rewarding, each of us must be able to routinely access the positive feelings and experiences that drew us to teaching in the first place. Just how to do this successfully is a major question for many teachers.

We believe that at least part of the answer to the question about longevity in teaching (i.e., why some teachers remain in the profession while

---

*Hussar, W. J. (2000). Predicting the need for newly-hired teachers in the United States to 2008–09. *Education Statistics Quarterly*, *1*(4). Retrieved February 8, 2007, from the National Center for Educational Statistics website, *http://nces.ed.gov/programs/quarterly/vol_1/1_4/3-esq14-g.asp#top*

**Data from the National Education Association website, "A better beginning: Helping new teachers survive and thrive," February 10, 2003. *www.nea.org/teachershortage/better-overview.html*

others leave) has to do with being able to seek and find what is at the heart of teaching. This process statement is not the same for each individual; in fact, quite the opposite is true. Both the process and the destination are unique for each person. Nevertheless, there are some commonalities. For most teachers the process of seeking the heart of teaching begins with mastering the outward trappings of teaching, such as implementing instructional tasks, designing and planning lessons, and managing classrooms. However, this is only part of the process. We believe that the more difficult part of the journey awaits us in the exploration of the inner world of teaching, such as learning about oneself in terms of personal values and beliefs, learning to interact effectively with the external world, and realizing that how one sees the world influences the choices one makes about teaching. We also believe that without an exploration of this inner world of teaching, it is difficult to maintain a positive experience of teaching over the long term.

Seeking the heart of teaching is both a journey and a destination. It is a journey because we are continually growing and changing in our roles as teachers and in our experience of teaching. The journey involves continuous reflection on the experiences we have of teaching and the use of strategies to maximize the positive impact these experiences can have on our lives. Seeking the heart of teaching is also a destination in that it can be described in terms of specific kinds of positive experiences that we seek for and desire from teaching. We want to reach a point in our professional lives in which the positive experiences of teaching predominate and the problems we may have had in the journey seem to arise much less frequently. In this book, we will share with you some practical ways to approach the journey and provide you with some ways to characterize your experience of the destination when you reach it.

## PROFESSIONAL AND PERSONAL LIVES

Teaching can tell us about ourselves if we are willing to recognize it as a catalyst for our own personal growth and development. We are not alone in the realization that teaching can contribute to our personal growth. Other scholars in the field also acknowledge this point of view.

And beyond a desire to increase the effectiveness of your teaching in technical or procedural terms, you are probably also attracted by the idea that there is a potential for connection between professional development and personal development. If you can become more aware of your own aptitudes, preferences, and strengths and use them in your teaching, you might not only develop your own best style of teaching, you might also develop as the type of person that you want to be. (Edge, 2002, p. 7)

Unfortunately, many teachers are not able to see teaching as an opportunity for personal growth and development. As Clarke noted at the beginning of the chapter, many teachers compartmentalize their lives as teachers, assuming a teacher persona in the classroom that may be strikingly different from the real persona used in daily life outside the classroom. We believe this tendency to compartmentalize is a typical response to the stress of teaching and working within educational systems. Teaching can be a frightening endeavor, and it can seem safer to be one person in the classroom—someone who may be less engaged, somewhat distant, and in control—and quite another person outside the classroom with people whom we know well. However, unless teachers can make the connection between their personal and professional lives, they will have difficulty exploring the inner world of teaching and in discovering what is at the heart of teaching for them.

Christison writes about her early experiences as a teacher in learning about the relationship between her personal and professional lives.

I think I had always wanted to be a teacher. As a young child I used to line up all of my dolls and stuffed animals in a row and pretend they were my students. In these pretend interactions, I was, of course, the perfect teacher and my dolls and stuffed animals were the perfect students. These pretend students were eager to learn whatever I chose to teach them. They were well behaved, learned everything quickly and easily, and were immensely respectful and grateful for the information I had to share. Naturally, it came as somewhat of a disappointment that teaching in my early days was not as highly rewarding as my pretend teaching situations had been. Part of my disappointment came from the idea that I could compartmentalize my life. I wanted everything to be perfect in the classroom. I was really two people: me the teacher and me everywhere else. I did not think that the two MEs were related or needed to be integrated in any way.

There was a reason for this. In the early 1980s, I went through a very unhappy time in my personal life. As a result, interaction with me was often inconsistent. It was during this time that I began to lose interest in teaching and found it difficult. I began to have conflicts with my students and found my interactions with colleagues stressful and unrewarding. When my students would ask me if I was all right, it would annoy me greatly. *Of course I was all right! I come to class on time; I'm always prepared, and papers are always returned promptly; I never (miss office hours, etc., etc.).* I believed then that my personal life and my personal development as an individual had no bearing on my teaching. Externally, I was manifesting the behaviors of what I thought a good teacher should be, but I did not feel very successful as a teacher. I thought seriously about leaving teaching altogether. It was a frustrating time for me.

I look back on this time in my professional life now and can clearly see the relationship between my personal and professional lives, but I could not see it then. I was not able to compartmentalize my life in the way that I imagined. I was unhappy and discouraged in my personal life, and no matter how hard I tried to do otherwise, and no matter how well I prepared or how creative my lessons were, this unhappiness and discouragement came through in my teaching and my interactions with my students and colleagues.

The process of making the connection between our personal and professional lives does not happen overnight. For us, the catalyst for recognizing that our personal lives could be so intimately connected to our professional lives came first from reading the ideas of others in education. In the mid 1970s and '80s we were fortunate enough to become acquainted with the works of some teacher educators (such as Stevick, 1976, 1980, 1982; Schön, 1983) who cast a broad net on teacher education, extending the vision of teaching beyond notions of theory and practice. In other words, these were educators who considered the relationship between the professional and personal lives of teachers and considered the whole person in teacher development. Their ideas started our thinking on this topic. Gradually we developed a view of our development as teachers that tied our professional lives to our personal lives as parents, as children, as friends, as partners, and as community activists.

## INTERNAL AND EXTERNAL WORLDS OF TEACHING

For most teachers, the early years of teaching are focused on the external world of teaching—that is, developing a knowledge base and a set of instructional strategies necessary to meet basic classroom and professional obligations. Teachers typically receive formal training in the external world of teaching: the information, skills, and systems that form the procedures for teaching in a classroom, such as learning how to write a syllabus, how to organize and present a lesson, how to deliver course content, how to test, how to grade, how to maintain a supportive learning environment, how to implement specific strategies for classroom management, and similar activities. However, as previously mentioned, we typically receive little, if any, formal training about the internal world of teaching: understanding ourselves and working effectively with this self-understanding. This quote from Jersild in Earl Stevick's groundbreaking book, *Memory, Meaning, and Method* (1976), makes exactly this point.

> A teacher cannot make much headway in understanding others or in helping others to understand themselves unless he is endeavoring to understand himself. If he is not engaged in this endeavor, he will continue to see those whom he teaches through the bias and distortions of his own unrecognized needs, fears, desires, anxieties, and hostile impulses. Jersild (1955, p. 4).

Figure 1.1 expresses our view of the connection between our internal and external worlds.

**Figure 1.1**   The Teacher's Internal and External Worlds

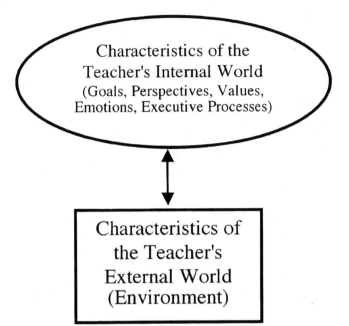

The characteristics of the internal world is the circle at the top. These characteristics, such as our true emotions, values, and goals, are often not directly observable. The characteristics of the external world is the box below the circle, and these characteristics represent anything in our environment that we can perceive through our senses, including people. The characteristics of the internal world interact with the characteristics of the external world, resulting in our experiences: how we perceive our relationship to the environment or how we feel about our teaching. To use a simple example, if a teacher tends to like outgoing people (a characteristic of the teacher's internal world) and ends up teaching a class full of extroverts (a characteristic of the teacher's external world), the interaction of these characteristics might result in the teacher's experience of enjoyment.

Palmer shares a brief example of how the internal and external worlds of teaching are interwoven.

A number of years ago, I taught a class that I had previously had enormous success with, but which had suddenly become a disaster. My course evaluations were about as bad as they could be, and I felt sad, disappointed, and angry in almost all parts of my life. A gray cloud hung over me. The first thing I did was to talk with some expert teachers about what had gone wrong. Clearly, part of the problem was that I had not responded to some changes in my external teaching environment. I had proceeded to teach my courses as I had done in the past while my teaching environment changed around me. For example, the composition of the student body had changed significantly—the student backgrounds and goals were different from past groups of students; yet, I had not responded to those changes. With the help of my advisors, we developed a new course with more cooperative learning, more group work, less material covered, more interactive activities and experiential learning, fewer lectures, and different evaluation procedures (e.g., portfolios versus formal tests). Implementing these changes made a huge difference. In my external world, my course evaluations improved greatly, and my students even expressed their appreciation for the course in its revised format. Internally, my anger and negativity subsided. I felt much better about my teaching and about life in general.

This story illustrates how the internal and external worlds work together or interact. The teacher had a difficult experience in the external world of teaching (i.e., receiving poor course evaluations). Naturally, this situation affected him internally (i.e., he felt sad, depressed, and angry as a result of his low student evaluations). It shows how working on his external world (i.e., the characteristics of his instruction) impacted his internal world (i.e., his thoughts and feelings about his teaching). The teacher also devoted considerable energy to working on changing specific (internal) attitudes that were affecting interaction with his students, and his students noticed a marked change as a result of this teacher's internal work.

## THREE EXPERIENCES OF THE DESTINATION

We believe there are three types of interactions that result in three different positive experiences that are at the heart of teaching. Each experience involves a different kind of interaction between characteristics of our internal world (what goes on inside us) and the characteristics of our external world (what happens around us). Most teachers have experienced these types of interactions at various times in their teaching. The goal is to experience teaching from one of these positive experiences as often as possible. We introduce the three types of experiences here, but we will return to them in subsequent chapters.

- *Type 1, Pleasure.* We experience pleasure when what is going on in our external world provides us with what we enjoy. So pleasurable teaching might provide the teacher with a comfortable working environment, interesting coworkers, a livable salary, decent working hours, and exciting travel. Therefore, pleasure is essentially enjoying what comes to us, what we receive.

- *Type 2, Satisfaction.* We experience satisfaction when we give to others a part of ourselves (i.e., we give what some people might call our personal talents or gifts) and receive appreciation for what we give. Satisfying work for a teacher might be giving his or her special abilities as a teacher and receiving the appreciation of the students. Thus, satisfaction is a two-way exchange: giving and receiving.

- *Type 3, Privilege.* We experience privilege when participating in our work feels like a once-in-a-lifetime opportunity in which we are lucky to be able to take part in. This type of experience is created entirely from within our internal world and is independent of any feedback from the external world. For example, a teacher might feel that it is a privilege just to know and interact with students. Thus, what distinguishes privilege from pleasure and satisfaction is that it derives only from giving.

## OVERVIEW OF MAIN TOPICS

The chapters of this book provide more detailed information on the possible connections between your personal and professional lives and between your internal and external worlds. We will focus on the different ways of responding to the external world so that you might predominantly experience teaching as one of the three types of positive experiences and ultimately find what is at the heart of teaching for you.

Chapter 2 provides a framework for organizing our thinking about the internal world by breaking it into a limited number of components. Subsequent chapters elaborate on the components by describing each one in detail and suggesting specific ways for developing and working with them. Chapter 3 addresses the role that affective schemata play and includes a discussion on the importance of managing emotions. Chapter 4 provides an overview of some basic communication principles and provides an introduction to the notion of internal perspectives. Chapter 5 operationalizes the communication principles in terms of specific communication strategies. Chapter 6 introduces the concept of teacher specialties: habitual ways of relating to the world that can either promote or interfere with the different types of experiences we may have. Chapters 7–9 focus on the roles of the higher-order executive processes in seeking the heart of teaching. Chapter 7 specifically addresses the use of the processes of reflection and goal setting, as well as values clarification, while Chapter 8 describes the role of planning to achieve goals. Chapter 9 provides specific strategies for implementing and evaluating one's plan. Finally, Chapter 10 explores ways to create harmony in a teacher's internal and external worlds.

We hope these chapters bring you closer to finding the heart of teaching for you.

# Chapter 2

# A Conceptual Framework for Seeking the Heart of Teaching

Chapter 1 made a case for the important role that knowledge of one's internal world and an understanding oneself plays in how we experience both our personal and professional lives as teachers. However, we are certainly not the first educators to recognize this fact. Jersild (1955) came to this conclusion a half a century ago, and Stevick (1976) reaffirmed it two decades later. Edge (2002) has also recognized the importance of both the external and internal worlds. However, most of the references to the internal world have referred to its importance, but have not attempted to characterize it. In this chapter, we present a conceptual framework for organizing our thinking about the components of the internal world. We also provide a way of conceptualizing the major functions of each of these components and discuss how they might interact with one another and with the external world. In the remainder of the book, we will elaborate on the characteristics of each component of the internal world and offer some guidance on how we might use this information in developing a rich and rewarding professional teaching life.

## CONCEPTUAL FRAMEWORK OF INTERNAL AND EXTERNAL WORLDS

### *Observable Variables and Constructs*

Before we present our framework for the inner world and describe its components, we need to digress a bit to make an important distinction between two fundamentally different types of components that we will use in the framework: observable variables and constructs. *Observable variables* are characteristics of objects that can be directly observed and measured. Many characteristics of the external world fall into this category, such as the gender of an individual, the height of an individual, the time of day, and the number of students in a classroom.

In contrast to observable variables, *constructs* name things that cannot be directly observed. A construct can be (1) an idea or a concept, not directly observable or measurable, such as a theory of intelligence; (2) a concept inferred from empirical data to explain a phenomenon, such as pragmatic knowledge inferred from performance on language tests; or (3) a definition of a concept that is manifested in other observable characteristics, such as the concept of *specialties* (to be defined later) as exhibited in behaviors observed under specific circumstances (Peng, Yeng, & Meuller, 2003, pp. 181–182).

Many of the components of the conceptual framework we will present are constructs. For example, when we attribute an emotion to an individual, we do so on the basis of our own notion or concept of what an emotion is and what we believe the basic categories of emotions are.

One observer might call an emotion anger while another might say that what is really going on with the same individual is actually two emotions: the surface emotion, anger, and a deeper underlying emotion, fear. If you were to ask the individual what he or she was experiencing, he or she might say one thing while a psychologist observing the individual might say another.

An individual can collect evidence to support an interpretation of emotional states by measuring observed variables (such as flushing of the skin or the amount of brain wave activity) and then use this evidence to support a hypothesis regarding the specific emotion being experienced. However, the observable evidence is not equal to the hypothesized emotion, and the observed evidence associated with the hypothesized emotion cannot be interpreted as indicating that the specific emotion exists or is a fact. At best, the observed evidence can only be taken as support for a hypothesis. Stating hypotheses about constructs as if they are facts takes one beyond the realm of science and gives the impression that one knows more than is actually knowable. Moreover, describing internal psychological states as facts can prevent an individual from seeking alternative interpretations that may actually better achieve the individual's goals. For example, if an individual is absolutely committed to a belief that a particular emotion he or she is experiencing (such as anger) is a fact, he or she may stop there and not even consider the possibility that he or she is also afraid. The point is that working with constructs is complex. While we need a framework to talk about the internal world of teaching, we ask you to remember that in our conceptual model, we are hypothesizing about internal constructs, not presenting these constructs as facts.

Figure 2.1 offers a conceptual framework for organizing our thinking about the internal and external worlds of a teacher. It expands Figure 1.1. The oval shows the hypothesized constructs of the internal world: goals, perspectives, specialties, values, affective schemata, and executive processes. The rectangle presents several important observable variables in the external world, including the physical characteristics of the external world, the individuals, time, and systems.

## SOME HYPOTHESIZED CONSTRUCTS OF THE INTERNAL WORLD*

Being aware of how the components of the internal world work is one way of knowing ourselves. In this framework, knowing ourselves involves knowing what our goals are, such as becoming a school principal, getting an advanced degree, etc. Being aware of our internal world also involves knowing what our values are, such as being kind to or honest with others. In addition, being aware of our internal world involves knowing about the different ways we can relate to different situations and individuals around us. We label these latter components perspectives and specialties. Because the way we use these terms may be unfamiliar to some teachers, we provide introductory information below on both of these concepts.

Knowing our emotional makeup and how our emotions affect our behavior are also part of being aware of our internal world. For example, we might know that we tend to overreact emotionally in certain situations, such as having our authority challenged, and that we do not make good decisions at these times. At the core of our internal world are the higher-order executive processes of reflection, goal-setting, planning, implementation, and evaluation—processes we use to make important decisions in our lives. These processes interact with the goals, values, specialties, and perspectives through our emotions or affective schemata. Of course, the components of the internal world also interact with the characteristics of our external world. Thus, it is possible that two individuals could respond very differently to the same event in the external world and have a very different internal experience of it. For example, two teachers may experience the same staff meeting very differently. How the teachers respond to the staff meeting is based on the differences in the components of their individual internal worlds, such as their goals, values, and affective schemata. In the interest of providing the clearest understanding of each of the components of the internal world more completely, we will briefly describe them.

**Figure 2.1**    Conceptual Framework for the Internal and External Worlds of Teaching*

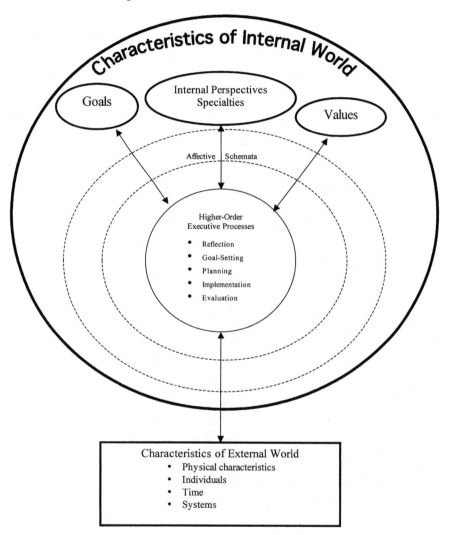

---

*The shape of Figure 2.1 and some of the thinking behind it can be found in Bachman and Palmer (1996). However, a number of the constructs are specific to Figure 2.1: goals, perspectives, specialties, and values. The constructs in the three ovals at the top of the figure can be thought of as an elaboration on the more general construct "personal characteristics" in Bachman and Palmer's framework for describing components of language use and language test performance (Bachman & Palmer, 1996, pp. 63–64).

### Goals

Goals are decisions we make about what we want to accomplish in life, such as graduating from college, getting a good job, or having kids someday. We all have goals, and they can influence how we behave and how we experience our lives. For example, if you want to get a better job, you might be motivated to stay up late at night studying for an exam to pass a class you need in order to graduate. In this book, Chapters 7 and 8 are devoted to goals.

### Internal Perspectives

*Internal perspectives* refer to the different emotional and cognitive ways one relates to various experiences in life. These varying internal perspectives also form a part of how you view your internal world. For example, let's say that you are having a discussion with colleagues. One colleague offers an opinion or makes a statement about students that you find very offensive. You would like to give her a piece of your mind, but in the interests of cooperation and collegiality, you refrain. Later, you mention your reaction to another colleague who was present when the offensive statement was made. She can hardly remember the comment and doesn't seem offended by it at all. Although you and your colleague witnessed the same event, you viewed it from a different perspective. Moreover, perspectives change. Your perspective may not only differ from your colleague's, but you may find that you view the event from a different perspective at a later date. Support for the notion of internal perspectives exists in both the scientific community and in the wider community of people who reflect on the human condition. In Chapter 4, we introduce five internal perspectives and show how understanding them is useful for improving communication with students and colleagues.

### Specialties

A *specialty* is a specific set of behaviors associated with a particular internal perspective. Specialties are behaviors that we have mastered and perform extremely well—hence the use of the word *specialty* to characterize these behaviors. Specialties help make up our persona—that is, the way we generally come across to others, especially our students and colleagues. We may or may not be aware of our specialties or the behaviors in our teaching associated with the specialties.

Because specialties are behaviors we do well, we may have a tendency to overuse them and use them in situations where they may be inappropriate. For example, a common specialty for teachers and educators is *Helpful.* (For the purposes of this book, the names of specialties [e.g., *Helpful*] will be capitalized and in bold italics.) A teacher with the specialty of *Helpful* often has a high energy level, has the ability to get things done, and is usually very involved with students. The weakness of this specialty in overuse is that the teacher may have an inability to slow down and pay attention to some aspects of personal life, such as interpersonal communication, family life, and maintaining health. We believe that specialties play a central role in finding long-term personal satisfaction in teaching and in being able to routinely experience teaching as satisfying, pleasurable, or as a privilege. Chapter 6 is devoted to specialties.

### *(Governing) Values*

The values we refer to in the conceptual model are actually governing values. *Governing values* are the most important principles by which we live our lives. They help define our concept of who we are. When used as the basis for decision-making, they help create rewarding experiences (including experiences of integrity) and guide the process in one's most important decision-making experiences. Examples of governing values include such statements as, "I am a caring parent," "I tell the truth," and "I appreciate diversity."

Governing values differ from individual to individual; what is important to one person may or may not be important to another. We must look within to discover our governing values and not judge them according to some external standard. Discovering governing values and using them to guide our actions is central to seeking the heart of teaching. We devote Chapter 7 to discovering governing values and how they influence us.

### Affective Schemata

*Affective schemata* are emotional correlates of experiences, including the topical knowledge of the world associated with those experiences. When we internalize knowledge of the world through experiences, we simultaneously internalize feelings associated with those experiences. Moreover, when we access knowledge of the world, we also access the feelings associated with the knowledge and with the circumstances under which the knowledge was internalized. For example, individuals from different racial backgrounds are likely to have different feelings associated with their knowledge of race and racial events and the circumstances under which they internalized this knowledge.

Affective schemata (i.e., feelings about knowledge or experiences) play an extremely important role in our behavior. On the positive side, feelings of enthusiasm and interest in knowledge, events, and relationships can motivate us to continue to be involved with that knowledge or those experiences. For example, let's take English grammar. If your first experience with learning about English grammar was highly positive (for example, if it was presented as an interesting game), you might continue to be involved in some way with English grammar, perhaps by developing it as an area of specialization. If your first experience was negative, the associated emotions might cause you to avoid experiences. For example, if in your first experience with learning English grammar you became angry with the instructor or you were confused by the material, it is unlikely that you would be involved in learning English grammar in the future unless you had a later positive experience of it. Because of the important role affective schemata play in the lives of teachers, we devote Chapter 3 to them.

### Executive Processes

The executive processes are the higher-order processes of reflection, goal-setting, planning, implementation, and evaluation.** The term *higher*

---

** Executive processes comprise only one set of mental functions, which also include cognitive strategies (Chamot & O'Malley, 1987). Cognitive strategies for learning include note-taking, applying rules, using target language resource materials, classifying, inferencing, and elaborating. Since this book is about how to get at the heart of teaching and not about how to teach per se, we do not deal specifically with cognitive strategies here.

*order* is associated with Bloom's Taxonomy (Bloom, 1956) in which he identifies different cognitive processes—knowledge, comprehension, application, analysis, synthesis, and evaluation. The final three processes in Bloom's taxonomy (i.e., analysis, synthesis, and evaluation) are considered higher-order cognitive skills that provide a cognitive management function and are necessary to performing the executive processes.

## Reflection

Reflection involves taking stock of characteristics both internal and external to the individual. As we have noted, internal characteristics include the goals, perspectives, specialties, values, affective schemata, and higher-order executive processes. Characteristics of the external environment include the physical characteristics, the people involved, time, and systems. If we take time to reflect on the characteristics of our internal and external worlds, we are more likely to make balanced and thoughtful decisions, thereby giving us greater satisfaction in our work. Reflection can be used prior to taking action, as precursor to goal-setting and planning, or it can be used after taking action when we want to think about what we have done and the consequences of our actions.

## Goal-Setting

In setting goals, the focus is on the process rather than the product. Setting goals involves specifying the outcomes you want to achieve. In Chapter 7, we suggest that setting goals is one of the three stages in the management of time. (The others, planning and implementation, are associated with achieving the goals you have set.) Goals must also be consistent with our values. Chapter 7 is devoted to the relationship between values clarification and setting of goals.

## Planning

Planning to achieve goals involves using our knowledge of the characteristics of our internal and external world to sequence tasks and develop a time frame for carrying them out in order to achieve our goals. For example, if a teacher has set a goal to raise the percentage of students passing an exam to a certain value, he or she must decide what tasks are required and prepare the supplementary material for the students. The teacher must also decide when to schedule time to accomplish these tasks. Chapter 8 is devoted to the importance of planning to achieve our goals.

### Implementation and Evaluation

Implementation involves carrying out tasks and tracking progress as the plan is being carried out. Evaluation involves determining how well goals have been achieved. Chapter 9 is devoted to the implementation and evaluation of goals.

## SOME CHARACTERISTICS OF THE EXTERNAL WORLD

The characteristics of the external world include the characteristics of the physical environment and the characteristics of the individuals in that environment. Also included in the characteristics of the external world are the use of both time and systems we have created and in which we work.

### *Physical Characteristics*

In the teaching domain, teachers interact with the physical environment as well as with the available resources, such as how much space they have in their classroom, what books and equipment they have at their disposal, how much money they make, and how much money is available to them for materials and supplies.

### *Individuals*

Teachers also interact with individuals: students, other teachers, supervisory staff, and members of the community. One of the most important ways teachers interact with individuals is through face-to-face communication. The characteristics of individuals in the external world can be described using the same constructs that we use to describe the internal world: goals, perspectives, specialties, values, and affective schemata. Since the focus of this book is primarily on the internal world of teaching, we will not provide much detail in describing the characteristics of individuals in the external world.

## Time

We also interact with the passage of time by the way we schedule it or otherwise spend it on specific tasks. We believe that the management of time is important in seeking the heart of teaching. We devote Chapters 7–9 to the management of time as it relates to the internal world or teaching.

## Systems

As teachers we interact with systems in both our professional and personal lives. For example, in our professional lives we interact with systems within the educational institution such as systems for admitting and placing students, systems for keeping track of student progress, and systems for grading. In our personal lives, we interact with systems for the management of time, money, and communication (phone, email, etc.).

In subsequent chapters, the characteristics of the internal world that we have identified in the conceptual framework (Figure 2.2) will be dealt with in depth, thus providing what Edge (2002) believes is needed for continued development: an internal growth approach. We believe it is through our internal growth that we find the heart of teaching.

# Chapter 3

# Affective Schemata

This chapter examines more closely the role that emotions (i.e., affective schemata) play in the internal world of teaching. Our discussion of
affective schemata in this chapter is focused on:

- providing a working definition of an emotion
- describing how affective schemata are encoded with environmental
  characteristics
- discussing the neurobiology of emotions
- defining the concept of emotional intelligence
- providing an overview of the concept of core or basic emotions

- explaining emotions in the context of the experience of *flow*
- discussing the role emotions play in the internal world of teaching

What are emotions? What is a definition of emotion that is helpful for teachers? We hope to provide some answers to these questions.

An extensive history surrounds the exploration of emotions. In the early third century BCE, the Greek philosopher Aristotle, in *Nicomachean Ethics*,* challenged his students to learn how to manage their emotional lives. Anyone can become angry—that is easy. But to be angry with the right person, to the right degree, at the right time, for the right purpose, and in the right way—this is not easy.

Two thousand years later, the French philosopher René Descartes** (1596–1650) speculated about the place of emotion as a mediator between a stimulus and a response. Since the early 17$^{th}$ and 18$^{th}$ centuries, many dictionaries have attempted to define an emotion (Candland, 1977, p. 4), and hundreds of philosophers and researchers have tried to create working definitions of an emotion (Ekman & Davidson, 1990). Unfortunately, the only common ground among a myriad of writers is that an emotion is not easy to define (Richins, 1997).

For our purposes, we will define an emotion as "a feeling and its distinctive thoughts, psychological and biological states, and range of propensities to act" (Goleman, 1995, p. 289). Some cognitive and developmental psychologists hold the view that the emotional correlates of events are encoded within us along with the physical, factual pieces of events themselves (Penfield, 1975). Elaborating on this notion, Schumann (1997) states that (affective) schemata are formed as analog memories of emotional experiences. . . . Affective aspects of. . .interactions are stored in the. . .memory along with the memory of the emotional experience accompanying these events (Schumann, 1997, p. 6 referencing Leventhal, 1984). Subsequently,

the schematic emotional memory provides an automatic appraisal of new stimulus events on the basis of past experience with similar situations. Such appraisals, which are often outside of consciousness, shape the

---

*See Sachs (2002) translations in the References.
**See Descartes (1637) with translation by Haldance and Ross (1970).

perception of events by coding the situation input into the emotional schemata themselves. Thus, previous experiences with noxious or pleasant stimuli are recorded in the schemata and then act as a filter allowing the organism to focus attention on and generate expectations about subsequent experiences. (Schumann 1997, pp. 6–7). (See also Ledoux, 1993; Cahill, Prins, Weber, & McGaugh, 1994.)

The interrelated nature of experiences and emotions is one reason why sorting out emotions and our emotional lives is so complex. We can feel out of control in certain situations because we are not only dealing with the emotional correlates of present experiences but with those of past experiences as well. For example, let's say that you are teaching a new course and that you love the subject matter and are well prepared to teach it. However, let's say that you have a bad experience teaching the course because of the presence of a small group of difficult students. They are loud, boisterous, contentious, and difficult. Their behavior interferes with learning and makes the class unpleasant. Based on this experience, chances are that, if you are asked to teach the course again to another group of students, your initial reaction will be a negative one. Therefore, if you are not aware of how your previous experience has been recorded in the affective schemata and is acting as a filter, that is generating negative expectations about subsequent experiences, you might make a decision to never teach the course again. And that could be a mistake and prevent you from finding a positive experience in teaching.

## THE NEUROBIOLOGY OF EMOTIONS

In order to understand the hold that emotions have on thinking and why it seems that reason and feelings are often in conflict with each other, it is important to understand how the brain functions relative to emotions and how it has evolved over thousands of years of evolution. All species that have more than a minimal nervous system have a brainstem at the top of the spinal column. This brainstem regulates basic life functions like breathing and heart rate, but it does not actually learn (Maclean, 1990). From this primitive brain, the emotional centers and the limbic system emerged. From the emotional centers, the thinking brain, or the neocortex, grew. If we look at the fact that the thinking part of the brain evolved from the emotional part of the brain, it helps us to understand the relationship of thought to feeling.

The emotional brain and the rational brain are closely intertwined. For example, a friend of ours was devastated when his wife of ten years died rather suddenly of cancer. Her death had come as a shock to him; he was saddened and distraught. About a year after her death, we had lunch with him. He told us that he was dating another woman that he really liked, that he was happy, and that he did not think about his wife. However, when he mentioned his wife's name, his eyes filled with tears, indicating that on some level he was still sad, despite his words to the contrary. His two brains, the emotional and the rational, were strongly connected to the events in his life, but each in a slightly different way.

One of the most exciting discoveries in recent years revealed how the amygdala can hijack the brain (LeDoux, 1986, 1991, 1993, 1994; Barinaga, 1992). In order to understand how this happens, it helps to remember a few basics of brain biology. Although the brain weighs only about two or three pounds and is only about the size of your two doubled fists, it uses up to 20 percent of the body's energy. This means that when the heart pumps blood, about twenty percent will go through the carotid arteries to the brain. This blood carries important nutrients such as glucose and oxygen. The brain needs both oxygen and glucose to stay healthy, and if the brain does not get enough glucose or enough oxygen, the results will be dramatic. You may feel like you cannot think clearly, you may feel lightheaded, and, in some cases, you may even lose consciousness if there is not a constant and even supply of oxygen and glucose.

Another important fact about the brain that is important for understanding the biology of emotions is that there are key functional areas of the brain. The brain is divided into different lobes—occipital, parietal, temporal, and frontal. Specific functions are centered in these different lobes, such as vision in the occipital lobe. The frontal lobe is responsible for the ability to solve problems and the logical processing of information. Another key functional area is in the center of the brain. Collectively, this center is called the limbic area and includes the amygdala, hypothalamus, thalamus, and hippocampus. The structures known as the amygdala (almond-shaped structures on each side of the brain) are particularly important in the biology of emotional intelligence because they are the seat of emotions (Jensen, 1998; Christison, 1997, 2006). Sensory signals from the eye or ear travel first to the thalamus and across a single synapse to the amygdala. A second signal from the thalamus follows and is routed to the neocortex. The branching of this signal allows the amygdala (the emotional center) to respond to a situation *before* the neocortex. In emotionally charged situations, we naturally respond from our emotional center first, before our frontal lobe has a chance to process the information (Goleman, 1998). This phenomenon is the reason why, in emotionally charged situations, we sometimes say things that we later regret or we cannot find the words to express what we want to say; the response is an emotional one rather than one that has been processed logically in the frontal lobe. Understanding the neural pathways for emotions helps explain how emotions are able to overwhelm reason.[3]

## EMOTIONAL INTELLIGENCE

### *Definition of Emotional Intelligence*

Emotional intelligence refers to "the capacity for recognizing our own feelings and those of others, for motivating ourselves, for managing emotions well in others, and in our relationships" (Goleman, 1995, p. 42–43; Salovey & Mayer, 1990, p. 189).[***] In his original framework, Gardner proposed two personal intelligences—the interpersonal and the intrapersonal intelligences.

> *Inter*personal intelligence is the ability to understand other people: what motivates them, how they work, how to work cooperatively with them. Successful salespeople, politicians, teachers, clinicians, and religious leaders are all likely to be individuals with high degrees of interpersonal intelligence. *Intra*personal intelligence . . . is a correlative ability, turned

---

[***]This definition stems from Gardner's original work (1983) on multiple intelligences.

inward. It is a capacity to form an accurate, veridical model of oneself and to be able to use that model to operate effectively in life. (Gardner, 1993, p. 9)

The concept of emotional intelligence was later expanded on by two of Gardner's colleagues at Harvard, Peter Salovey and John Mayer, who proposed a specific model of Emotional Intelligence (Salovey & Mayer, 1990). Emotional intelligence is distinct from but complementary to academic intelligence, "the purely cognitive capacities measured by IQ (Goleman, 1995, p. 42–43).

People from all walks of life are beginning to realize that success in the workplace environment takes more than intellectual excellence, technical or physical prowess, and subject matter expertise (Goleman, 1998, p. 12).

We need to develop emotional intelligence to survive in any workplace environment and certainly to develop positive interactions and communication with our fellow coworkers and our students.

### *Importance of Emotional Intelligence for Educators*

Recent studies indicate that children are achieving higher and higher IQ scores; yet, their emotional intelligence is on the decline. In a 1989 study by Achenbach and Howell (as referenced in Goleman, 1998, p. 12), two random samples of American children, ages 7 to 16, were evaluated by adults who knew them well. The first group was assessed in the mid-1970s and the second group in the mid-1980s. The rate of decline in students' emotional intelligence was found to be the same across all economic groups. Moreover, Achenbach and Howell believe that the decline in children's basic emotional competence is worldwide (Goleman, 1998, p. 12). What this trend portends for the workplace in the future is troubling at best, so what can be done to reverse it?

The answer to this question brings us face-to-face with the reason why emotional intelligence is important for educators: If we are to be successful as educators, we must develop our own emotional intelligence, which, according to Goleman (1995), is a matter of mastering our skills in the areas of self-awareness, self-management, self-motivation, and handling of relationships. Moreover, as teachers, we must understand the process of developing emotional intelligence well enough to guide our students in developing their own (Goleman, 1995, 1998; Sternberg, 1985). In order to develop our own emotional intelligence and to help our students in developing theirs, we need some understanding about what emotions are, how they are wired in the body, and what process and/or strategies we can use to work with emotions effectively.[2] In the Appendix, you will find an EQ (Emotional Intelligence Quotient) Inventory (p. 195) to help you understand your own EQ and to help you further develop your EQ in the areas identified by Goleman.

## CORE EMOTIONS

Hundreds of words are used to refer to emotions, but some theorists find it useful to propose a small set of core emotions from which all other emotions are derived. We have found this reductive process useful because working with a limited set of emotions provides a useful conceptual framework for organizing our thinking about emotions. With a manageable framework we are more likely to use the information to further our understanding of emotions, including particular emotions that either support or hinder us in accomplishing our goals.

### Research Evidence for Core Emotions

The argument for a set of core or basic emotions hinges to some extent on the early research of Levenson, Ekman, and Friesen (1990). These researchers garnered support for a set of basic emotions by noticing that specific facial expressions for fear, anger, sadness, and happiness are recognized by people in cultures throughout the world. Ekman (1999, 2003) continued this research on basic emotions and expanded and refined his early thinking to include specific ways in which emotions are different from one another. His list is quite lengthy, and a complete review of his work is beyond the scope of this book. Therefore, we have limited our discussion to three of the ways these basic emotions are different from one another because this information is most germane to the work we do as educators. The specific differences in emotions that Ekman discusses are (1) how emotions influence our ability to appraise antecedent events, (2) how they provoke probable behavioral responses, and (3) how they trigger certain physiological responses in the body.

First, let us consider how emotions influence our ability to appraise antecedent events. For example, if you are angry as a result of an event that just occurred, your appraisal of that event would be different from your appraisal of that same event if you were happy as a result. Let us say a student has a problem with a grade you have given her on a midterm exam. She approaches you after class, asking you to raise her grade. If the class went well and you are feeling good, you are more likely to respond to her request in an open and helpful manner. If the class did not go well and you are feeling somewhat agitated, you are more likely to respond to her request in a negative way. The current event (i.e., the student's request for a grade change) is influenced by your feelings toward the antecedent event (i.e., the events that took place during your class or events that may have taken place with that student).

Another way in which basic emotions are different from one another is that they provoke probable behavioral responses. Most of us would say that we respond individually and uniquely to emotions. Although behavioral responses differ from person to person (e.g., we cannot say that all people slam doors when they are angry or that all people cry when they are sad), each person usually has a specific way of responding to an emotion that is unique for them, and the way each person responds to anger is generally the same, no matter the occasion. Yet, each of us may respond differently to anger.

Finally, emotions are also distinct physiologically from one another, and these physiological changes associated with emotions prepare us to respond to different emotional states. New technologies helping us measure various physical changes provide us with more detailed information on brain biology and help us fine-tune these distinctions.[3] For example, with happiness there is increased activity in the brain, but with sadness there is a drop in brain activity (Goleman, 1995; Levenson, Ekman, & Friesen, 1990). Further, Goleman's research (1998) indicates that when a person is experiencing anger, blood flows to the hands, heart rate increases, and a rush of hormones generates a pulse of energy strong enough for vigorous action. With fear, blood flows to the large skeletal muscles, and blood is shunted away from the face. A flood of hormones puts the body on general alert. With happiness there is increased activity in the brain center. This activity inhibits negative feelings and fosters an increase in energy. The individual feels less worried and troubled. When a person feels sadness, there is a drop in energy and enthusiasm for life. Through the use of new technologies, researchers are discovering more physiological details of how emotions are different from one another.

### Descriptions of Core Emotions

Based on the work of Ekman (1999, 2003), Goleman outlines a list of seven core emotions with subcategories of emotions. These seven core or basic emotions differ from each other in at least the ways mentioned and provide a useful taxonomy for anyone working with emotions and developing emotional intelligence.

- **Anger:** fury, outrage, resentment, wrath, exasperation, indignation, vexation, acrimony, animosity, annoyance, irritability, hostility, hatred, and at the extreme, violence
- **Sadness:** grief, sorrow, cheerlessness, gloom, melancholy, self-pity, loneliness, dejection, despair, and at the extreme, depression
- **Enjoyment:** happiness, joy, relief, contentment, bliss, delight, amusement, pride, sensual pleasure, thrill, rapture, gratification, satisfaction, euphoria, whimsy, ecstasy, and at the extreme, mania
- **Love:** acceptance, friendliness, trust, kindness, affinity, devotion, adoration, infatuation
- **Surprise:** shock, astonishment, amazement, wonder
- **Disgust:** contempt, disdain, scorn, abhorrence, aversion, distaste, revulsion
- **Shame:** guilt, embarrassment, chagrin, remorse, humiliation, regret, mortification, and contrition

Being able to recognize emotions is an important part of developing emotional intelligence. For example, one of the values of identifying a set of core emotions may be that it is simply easier to recognize and work with a set of seven core emotions than a paradigm that includes 40 or 50 emotions. Another value may be that the greater our ability to identify a range of emotions is, the less frightening these emotions are likely to appear to us (i.e., the familiar is likely to be less threatening than the unfamiliar).

### Core Emotions and Generating Flow

The concept of core emotions has been used by Csikszentmihalyi (1997) in his work with the concept of *flow*, which we believe has particular relevance to teaching. According to Csikszentmihalyi, *flow* experiences can be described as those times when there is a "sense of effortless action." Csikszentmihalyi's model is provided in Figure 3.1.

Csikszentmihalyi hypothesizes that *flow* is an emotional state that results from using high-level skills when participating in activities that are

**Figure 3.1**   Csikszentmihalyi's Model

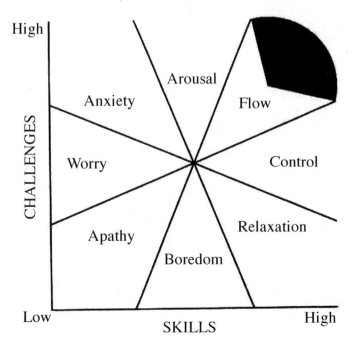

*Sources:* Adapted from Massimini & Carli, 1988; Csikszentmihalyi, 1990.

challenging (see the upper right-hand corner of Figure 3.1). For example, anxiety is an emotional state that can be very common during the first few years of teaching. Anxiety is a difficult state to be in for long periods of time since it is often associated with uncomfortable physiological sensations such as rapid heart rate, nausea, and inability to focus. According to Csikszentmihalyi's model, anxiety develops because of the particular relationship between the skills we have in a particular situation and the challenges we face. If the skills we possess for dealing with a particular situation are quite low and the challenges are quite high, the resulting emotional state is anxiety. However, notice what happens when the skills increase and the challenge remains high in the model: We then move into a state of flow. A common experience of flow occurs when skilled readers are left to read something that is intensely interesting in an environment conducive to silent reading. Most of us know that if left uninterrupted for long periods of time, we are often surprised to learn that so much time has passed. In such a situation, the skills a person has as a reader and the challenges one faces in reading are well matched. In other words, flow tends to occur when a person's skills are fully involved in overcoming a challenge that is just about manageable (Csikszentmihalyi, 1997, p. 30–31).

Flow also has two additional characteristics important for teachers to consider in thinking about how to create the experience of flow in a classroom setting. First, flow is likely to occur when someone faces a clear set of goals that require appropriate responses. When teachers ask students to set learning goals for themselves and also ask them to determine how to achieve the goals, they are creating an environment in which flow is more likely to occur. Second, flow is likely to occur when feedback is given quickly and when students are very clear on how well they have done on a particular task. Measures of formal feedback that occur as part of the instruction are also important in creating an environment in which flow is likely to occur. When none of the three characteristics of flow mentioned are present in a task or activity, it will be difficult for students to experience flow. (Massimini & Carli, 1988; Csikszentmihalyi, 1990 & 1996).

### Applying the Principles of Flow

Keeping the basic principles and components of flow in mind, we have developed a checklist for teachers to use in evaluating tasks that face them in their professional lives in terms of their potential for creating the experience of flow. This checklist can be used not only in formal, directed settings (such as a seminar for new teachers) but also as an instrument for use in developing one's own reflective practice. The chart outlines the components of a task essential for flow to occur.

| Components of a Task Necessary for Flow | Rating Scales (from low to high) | | | | |
|---|---|---|---|---|---|
| | 1 | 2 | 3 | 4 | 5 |
| 1. The goals have been clearly identified. | | | | | |
| 2. I know exactly what I need to do to achieve the goals. | | | | | |
| 3. I am getting feedback quickly. | | | | | |
| 4. I am getting useful feedback. | | | | | |
| 5. I know how well I am doing. | | | | | |
| 6. I believe my skills are being challenged by the task. | | | | | |
| 7. I have the skills to complete the task and achieve the goal. | | | | | |

To use this instrument, teachers rate themselves 1–5 on each of the components of the task that contributes to flow. If teachers consistently rate themselves at the top end of the scale, there will be more potential for flow to occur in the task. Using this instrument, teachers can also reflect on how to modify the task in order to achieve flow.

One of our colleagues recently shared an experience he had with flow. He noticed that during the spring semester, when he taught several classes, all with large numbers of students, and had a number of publishing deadlines to meet, he felt happy and energized despite the amount of work he had on his plate. He greatly enjoyed both the experience of work—preparing for class, teaching, and writing—and the outcomes—completing a variety of tasks and meeting deadlines. He woke up in the morning feeling positive about getting in to the office and tackling the tasks that faced him. When the summer vacation began, he felt less pressure and reduced involvement in his work. However, in doing so, he also noticed that he felt less satisfied than he had during the semester. After learning about the concept of flow, he realized that during the semesters he was often in a state of flow because his work life was centered on setting goals and determining how to achieve them, trying new concepts and ideas in his teaching and getting feedback from his students. The challenges he faced in his work life were also well matched to his skills and abilities. During vacation time, these characteristics were not so much a part of his work life. He set few goals and got little feedback on his work and writing. In essence, the characteristics of his work life that are associated with flow were no longer present in his day-to-day routines.

## THE ROLE OF EMOTIONS IN THE CONCEPTUAL FRAMEWORK FOR THE INTERNAL WORLD

Figure 2.1 in Chapter 2 (p. 14) presented a conceptual framework for the internal world of teaching that included affective schemata, or the emotional component of the model. In this framework, affective schemata (the emotional correlates of our experiences) influence how we use higher-order executive processes (i.e., our abilities to reflect, set goals, plan, implement plans, and evaluate plans) to affect how we interact with the external world. Thus, affective schemata can either facilitate or inhibit the use of the executive processes. So far, we have devoted much of our discussion on affective schemata to the experience of flow, showing how the affective schemata can facilitate positive experiences in the external world. However, affective schemata can also inhibit the use of the executive processes in teachers' professional and personal lives.

### Emotional Hijacking

Emotional hijacking occurs when the blood supply is momentarily diverted from the neocortical areas in the brain to the amygdala, the seat of emotions. If we interpret this biological process through the conceptual framework we propose, the affective schemata get energized and take control of behavior, bypassing the executive processes of reflection, goal-setting, planning, implementation, and evaluation. We represent this process in Figures 3.2a and 3.2b, as adaptations of Figure 2.1.

Figure 3.2a represents interaction without emotional hijacking. Under this condition, the arrow *through* the affective schemata shows that all of the following are involved in the student's interaction with the environment: executive processes, values, perspectives, strengths, and goals. (The affective schemata do not act as a filter to block access to the executive processes, goals, perspectives, etc.) Figure 3.2b represents interaction with emotional hijacking taking place. Under this condition, the arrow from the affective schemata to the external world shows that the affective schemata control the interaction and, in effect, filter or block the involvement of the executive processes, values, perspectives, strengths, and goals. The affective schemata interact directly with the characteristics of the external world (environment) to the relative exclusion of the individual's values, goals, perspectives, specialties, and executive processes.[4]

This shift of the locus of control from the executive processes to the affective schemata has two consequences: (1) preexisting goals, values, and plans get abandoned, and (2) the ability to create intelligent goals and plans is temporarily lost. Here is an example of these consequences: A teacher has planned to spend Saturday morning preparing for classes for the following week. On his way to the office he passes a department store and notices some interesting new clothes in the window. He suddenly feels the urge to shop and spends several hours happily buying new clothes. Tired from this activity, he feels the urge to take a long nap. After waking up from the nap and having a late lunch, he feels like it is now too late in the day to get started on class preparation, so he goes to watch a professional football game at the neighborhood sports bar. Well-laid plans to prepare for class preparation have been abandoned, precipitating a crisis management situation when the teacher no longer has time to do a good job preparing for classes the next week. Awareness of the fact that affective schemata play an important role in executive processing is crucial since effective planning is best done when one is not driven by one's emotions. Moreover, affective

**Figure 3.2a**    Without Emotional Hijacking

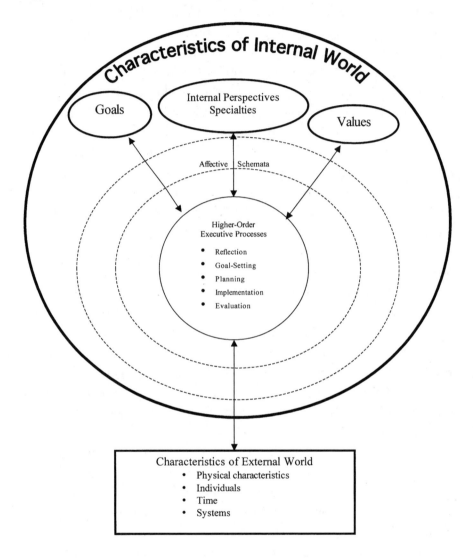

**Figure 3.2b**    With Emotional Hijacking

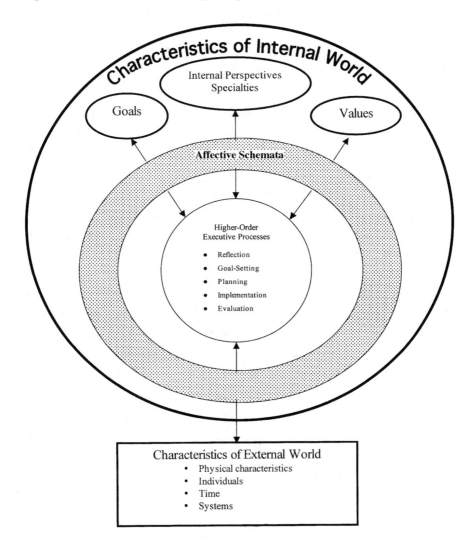

schemata also play an important role in the execution of one's plan since emotions can easily interfere with carrying out a well-thought-out plan.

Understanding a conceptual framework on paper can be much easier and more straightforward than working with this same framework in real-life situations. In fact, understanding emotional responses to situations can be tricky, especially in teaching environments and especially if we spend a lot of time in intellectual tasks involving sifting and sorting through data and looking at relationships between ideas. One reason that working with emotions in real-life situations can be so difficult is that emotional hijacking can be associated with a variety of symptoms, all of which are ultimately associated with the process depicted in Figure 3.3b, characterized as *emotion-backed demands* (Keys, 1975). The following list of types of emotion-backed demands is not meant to be exhaustive but is simply a reference to several types of symptoms.

### *Feeling* Symptom

This type of emotion-backed demand is accompanied by a physical *feeling* in the body. For example, suppose you are afraid of criticism. If you think that you might be criticized by some students because of how you have graded an exam, you may have feelings of fear (e.g., a sinking feeling in your stomach, a prickling feeling on your skin, a rush of blood to your head) just by thinking about the situation. This feeling may be so overwhelming that you may fail to implement your well-thought-out grading plan and even misuse your time in class because you don't want to engage or interact with your students.

### *Have to* Symptom

In this symptom, emotions masquerade in the guise of *have to* statements we construct in our minds. These statements usually contain the modal auxiliaries *must* or *have to* such as, *I must make this phone call, I have to finish my email,* or *I must not watch TV.* This type of emotion-backed demand often appears to be coming from our logical processing center but, in fact, does not involve logic.**** When this type of emotion-backed demand

---

****In Chapter 10, endnote 4, we discuss this symptom under the topic "contaminated ego states."

arises, the ability to be flexible and make good decisions about how to manage one's life is diminished since the emotion-backed demand looms as the only acceptable alternative (e.g., *I must make this phone call; I have to answer my email*).

*Have to* emotion-backed demands prevent completion of the tasks one has planned to accomplish. They also prevent making rational plans to accomplish needed or highly valued tasks. For example, all of us have had the best of plans to grade papers be sabotaged by a sudden feeling that cleaning the house, making phone calls, reading the paper, or even going shopping "just can't wait." The most common way to recognize this type of emotion-backed demand is recognizing the inability to find any convincing logical reason for yielding to the demand. Why do you need to make the phone call immediately? Clean the house? Go shopping? Answer your email?

### Unexamined Masquerade Symptom

This type of emotion-backed demand is driven by *unexamined* thoughts or reasons that give the appearance of having been logically thought out but which, in fact, have not. Moreover, such apparently logical reasons are almost always used repeatedly. Unexamined logical masquerades are often used by individuals who consider themselves logical and believe they relate to the world through thinking more than through feeling. In fact, one way to recognize this form of emotion-backed demand is through the presence of an ironclad logical justification. For example, let's say that one faculty member believes it is important to hold faculty meetings on Friday because it is difficult to find any other weekday when all the faculty members have free time. This judgment may be given before any attempt has been made to determine when faculty members are actually free. Individuals who have a strongly entrenched governing value associated with logic but who have not developed their emotional intelligence are particularly susceptible to the unexamined, masquerade-type of emotion-backed demand.

In this chapter on affective schemata, we laid out a framework for thinking about emotions and the role they might play in finding a satisfying and rewarding life as a teacher. As you are introduced to the remaining chapters, consider the role that emotions play in each one. In

Chapter 4, consider how emotions figure into internal perspectives and the outcomes of communication events. In Chapter 5, think about how specific communication strategies can be used to manage your own emotions and influence the emotions of others. In Chapter 6, focus on the role that emotions play in developing teacher specialties, and in Chapters 7–9, consider emotions and their influence on your use of time and how you employ the executive processes of reflection, goal-setting, planning, implementation, and evaluation.

Understanding and managing emotions is a complex task; yet, this task is certainly important for success in teaching since we are judged by a yardstick that includes more than just how much we know about our subject matter and more than our degrees, training, and expertise. Gone are the days when educators and teachers could simply lecture to a class and go home, almost ignoring any interaction with their students on a large scale. We must now think about our relationships with the students and the many other responsibilities that go hand-in-hand with teaching. Mastery of the content is only part of what we need to be successful professional educators. Personal qualities, such as initiative, adaptability, empathy with other people's situations, the ability to get along with students and colleagues, handling ourselves in difficult situations, skills in working in teams, and taking leadership responsibilities are all essential elements of success.

## NOTES

1. For an extended examination of the neurobiology of affect in language, including the neural system for stimulus appraisal, see Schumann (1997).

2. See Elias et. al (1997) for a comprehensive, integrated program of social and emotional education. The authors are members of the Research Group of the Collaborative for the Advancement of Social and Emotional Learning (CASEL).

3. Some of these new technologies include Positron Emission Tomography (PET scans), electroencephalogram (EEG), magneto-encephalography (MEG), magnetic resonance imaging (MRI), fMRI (functional magnetic resonance imaging), and NMRI (Nuclear Magnetic Resonance Imagery). PET reads the amount of glucose utilization or radioactive substances released when certain areas of the brain consume glucose. EEG gives us readings about the electrical output of the brain. MEG uses high-tech, super-cooled, liquid helium sensors to locate

faint magnetic fields generated by the brain's neural networks. MRI machines provide high-quality, cross-sectional images of soft tissue in the brain without X-rays or radiation. fMRI is a lower-budget variation that is cheaper and much faster. NMRI is 30,000 times faster and captures an image every 50 milliseconds. That speed can measure the sequence of thinking across very narrow areas of the brain.

4. When this blocking function of the affective schemata takes place, the schemata have been said to function as an *affective filter* (Dulay & Burt, 1977). When activated, the filter, represented by a grayed ring around the executive processes, blocks the operation of other components of the individual's internal world. For the first use of the term *affective filter* that we are aware of, see Dulay and Burt (1977). Stevick (1976) also discusses the idea of defensiveness blocking the access of input in a second language to an internal language acquisition device. Krashen (1981, p. 29–32) provides an early review of research relevant to the affective filter hypothesis and the role of affect in second language learning. This Affective Filter Hypothesis plays an important role in Krashen's theory of second language acquisition. The general form of Figure 2.1 (and Figures 3.2a and 3.2b) was developed by Bachman and Palmer (1996) with this metaphor of an affective filter in mind.

# Chapter 4

# Internal Perspectives and Communication Principles

We have introduced our conceptual framework for thinking about the internal world of teaching and that there are two important principles that govern our internal world: (1) be aware of our internal resources (i.e, our goals, perspectives, specialties, values, and affective schemata), and (2) be able to use our higher-order executive processes to make intelligent use of our resources. As discussed, key among our internal resources as teachers are what we call *internal perspectives,* which play an important role in developing the conceptual framework for our inner world, further our understanding of basic communication principles, and influence how we communicate with students and colleagues. An understanding of internal perspectives can also provide us with some ways of predicting and influencing the outcomes of communication.

Communication is an obvious concern for teachers. We communicate with students and colleagues as a part of our everyday work, and we want our interpersonal communications with students and colleagues to be successful. When we first started thinking about improving interpersonal communication, we focused solely on strategies for improving communication in the traditional sense. While we continue to believe that these communication strategies are important, our many years of experience and a great deal of study have convinced us that developing effective interpersonal communication involves much more than just learning and using a set of strategies; effectiveness in communication really results from the nature of our internal world (rather than being a natural consequence of events in the external world). Therefore, in this chapter we focus on learning more about our internal world—namely, internal perspectives—so that we can understand how this piece of the internal world influences communication in the external world. Making sense of this process will help us address a question most teachers consider paramount: What can we do to transform our internal world in ways that will improve our abilities to communicate with students and colleagues?

## MULTIPLE INTERNAL PERSPECTIVES: A FRAMEWORK

We use the term *internal perspectives* to refer to different emotional and cognitive ways that humans can relate to events in life. These varying perspectives form a part of how we view our internal world.[1] That an individual can be thought of as a composite of different internal perspectives may be new to you, so we introduce support for the idea of different internal perspectives both from the scientific community (Schwartz, 1995) and from the wider community of people who reflect on the human condition. Our experience with the concept of different internal perspectives is that most teachers who have been introduced to these ideas can identify them easily and quickly.

For example, let's say you are trying to decide whether or not to attend a professional meeting. You might make your decision analytically: What would it cost? How much work would I have to make up when I returned? You might also consider it from the perspective of whether it would further your progress in achieving particular goals, such as career advancement, intellectual development, or social networking. Would this count toward career development points? What new concepts would I learn that would help me in my teaching? Finally, you might consider it from the perspective of how it would feel to attend. Would attending this conference be fun, stimulating, boring? In fact, all of these perspectives may be present in your internal decision-making process. The framework we present in this chapter will give you a way to organize your thinking about different internal perspectives of this sort.

Over the years, psychologists have found it useful to conceive of the "self" as a collection of different internal parts, rather than a single unified entity—a single "I," as it were. Freud (1923/1962) divided the self into three parts: the Id, Ego, and Superego. Jung (1964) divided it into six internal archetypes: the Shadow, the Anima or Animus, the Synergy, the Child, and the Self. Gestalt psychology (Perls, 1973; Fagen & Shepherd, 1970) divided it into two parts: top dog and underdog. Voice Dialog (Dyak and Perot, 1999) divided it into a much a more extended set of parts.[2]

In addition to psychological views on multiple perspectives, others have also referred to these ideas in different contexts. For example, mythologist Joseph Campbell focused some of his scholarly interest in mythology and the human condition on the topic of multiple internal perspectives. In his view, evidence of the various internal perspectives goes back as far as ancient images of myth. In fact, Campbell theorized that the same set of great mythological voices that reoccur in cultures around the world are actually internal perspectives that get projected on the culture's interpretation of the external world. According to Campbell, "The images of myth are reflections of the spiritual potentialities in every one of us. Through contemplating these, we evoke their powers in our own lives" (Campbell, 1988, p. 207). Following is an example of how Campbell personally came to see the external images of myth as outward representations of *internal perspectives*.

When I was a little boy being brought up as a Roman Catholic, I was told I had a guardian angel on my right side and a tempting devil on my left, and that the decisions I made in life would depend on whether the devil or the angel had the greater influence upon me. As a boy, I concretized these thoughts, and I think my teachers did, too. . . .But instead of regarding them as facts, I can now think of them metaphors for the <u>impulses that move and guide me</u>. (Underline emphasis is the authors'.) (Campbell, 1988, p. 208).[3]

In addition to insights from the fields of psychology and mythology, many ordinary language expressions make reference to multiple perspectives, and we routinely use these expressions to describe our everyday experiences.

"I'm being hard on myself."

"I'm beating myself up."

"I make myself write."

"I force myself to exercise."

"I'm judging myself."

"I'm of two minds about that."

"Part of me wants to do X, and part of me wants to do Y."

"I get in my own way."

"I'm battling my demons."

"I'm conflicted."

"I made a half-hearted effort."

"I'm not going to try to fool myself."

"I talked myself into it."

"I convinced myself to do X."

"I promised myself to do X."

"I don't want to do this, but I have to."

We have all probably used or heard our students use a version of the last expression in this list, "I don't want to study for this exam, but I have to." A multiple internal perspective interpretation of this statement would attribute the statement to two different internal perspectives: one part of the student who just wants to play and the other part who feels responsible for studying. If the student actually ended up studying for the exam, the "I have to" perspective would prevail over the "I don't want to" perspective.

## TRANSACTIONAL ANALYSIS AND MULTIPLE PERSPECTIVES

The version of different internal perspectives that we have chosen to work with comes from transactional analysis.* In transactional analysis, the self is conceptualized as a collection of three internal ego states associated with memories of the primary figures in our lives as we are forming our views of the world: the child's own perspective, the perspective of a parent (as constructed by the child), and the perspective of an emotionally uninvolved adult (as constructed by the child). In transactional analysis, the Parent and Child ego states are further divided into two forms each, the Supportive and Critical Parent and the Natural and Adapted Child.

We use the term *internal perspectives* rather than the more traditional *ego states* because it is our experience that for many people the word *ego* carries with it a specific meaning, such as "self absorbed," which can have a negative connotation. *Perspective*, on the other hand, is relatively neutral. In addition, we use the five perspectives to further our understanding of teaching specialties (see Chapter 5).

Like other educators and psychologists, we have found transactional analysis to be relatively easy to apply. In fact, Roberts (1975, p. 2) noted that "the fact that it is easily understood and quickly related to personal relationships accounts for a large part of the increasing popularity of the approach." Goldhaber and Goldhaber (1976, p. 12) also indicated that "by studying and applying the principles of Transactional Analysis people can help themselves achieve greater personal awareness and possible behavior

---

*A student and friend of ours, Al Vrabel, first introduced us to transactional analysis in the 1970s.

change." While we emphasize that the version of transactional analysis that we present here is less complex than the versions that appear in the source literature, we believe this simplification is justified because both teachers and teacher educators need a system that is compact enough to internalize and work with.[5] We also believe that these internal perspectives are easy to recognize within all of us.

### Adult Perspective

The Adult perspective deals with the facts of current reality and with the unemotional process of objective decision-making and information processing (Goldhaber & Goldhaber, 1976, p. 37): "The function of the Adult perspective is to deal with presenting situations in an organized, adaptable, and intelligent way—in other words, reality testing" (Roberts, 1975, p. 13). The Adult perspective can remain detached and not become emotionally involved in any given situation. In a sense, the Adult perspective is like a computer, gathering and processing information and operating efficiently and consistently.

The language of the Adult can be quite complex. It is objective in nature and includes analytic statements of probability, similarity and differences, strengths and weaknesses, cause and effect, and description, which correspond to some of the rhetorical modes in expository writing (McCrimmon, 1984; Hunt, 1984). It asks for details and is completely non-judgmental and impersonal. A teacher operates from an Adult perspective in the classroom when lecturing to provide information, when analyzing student work without judgment and with an eye toward improvement, and when discussing strengths and weaknesses objectively.

### Supportive Parent Perspective

The function of the Supportive Parent perspective within the individual is to provide a set of values and standards for behavior for the individual and, therefore, to conserve energy and diminish anxiety. While the supportive Parent basically "has no fun" (Roberts, 1975, p. 12), it does serve to help the Child perspective (discussed on pp. 49–51) within the individual achieve its goals. Feelings associated with the Supportive Parent perspective include experiences of satisfaction and contribution.

The language of the Supportive Parent is inclusive (e.g., *How about if we. . .* versus *You should. . . .*). It provides reasons for directives. The Supportive Parent perspective can agree or disagree but does not approve or disapprove (i.e., language functions associated with judgment).

There are many occasions in teaching for the Supportive Parent perspective to make its own particular contribution. For example, when a student is having difficulty, a teacher often chooses to act supportively to help the student achieve his or her objectives. The teacher can also create opportunities for the students to experience the contribution of their own internal Supportive Parent perspective by providing opportunities for students to take responsibility in setting goals and making plans for achieving those goals. Students who assume the role of a supervisor or leader during group work are also using their Supportive Parent perspectives. When operating from the Supportive Parent perspective, students can support group members in achieving their goals and the goals of the group as a whole.

### Critical Parent Perspective

The Critical Parent is generally described in negative terms. Behaviors associated with the Parent's critical perspective include punishing, evaluating, hurting, and ridiculing, as well as being prejudiced, condescending, authoritarian, dictatorial, rigid, or closed-minded (Goldhaber & Goldhaber 1976, p. 35). While we describe the Critical Parent in similar terms, we interpret the behavior associated with the Critical Parent neutrally, recognizing that there is value in all of the behaviors and all of the different perspectives make important contributions.

With respect to language, the Critical Parent issues ultimatums (e.g., *You must. . .*) and can be highly critical (e.g., *You're stupid; you're lazy!*). This perspective can also blame (e.g., *How could you be so thoughtless, you idiot?*) and asks questions with embedded judgments (e.g., *Why aren't you more assertive? Why are you such a wimp?*). The critical Parent perspective uses verbs such as *should, must, ought to, have to, need to,* and the performative verb *disapprove.* The

Critical Parent perspective feels no need to provide reasons to the Child perspective that make sense and appeal to the intelligence and experience of the Child perspective.

There are many occasions in teaching for behaviors associated with the Critical Parent to surface. For example, a teacher may lecture from a superior, know-it-all, or patronizing position. A teacher may also act in a Critical Parental capacity by reprimanding or judging a students' behavior or performance. Teachers who interact with students from a Critical Parent perspective often experience themselves as separate from those whom they judge or criticize.

There are also a number of opportunities for students to experience the Critical Parent perspective. Once such opportunity occurs for some students when they are filling out anonymous course evaluations. In this situation, students often feel free to criticize an instructor because of the lack of any personal consequences to them. Another opportunity for students to experience the Critical Parent perspective results when teachers create a class environment in which students are encouraged to judge each other's oral or written work.

### Natural Child Perspective

The Natural Child perspective is spontaneous and energetic and has the ability to have fun with itself and others. The Natural Child perspective is also very intuitive and is a source of humor. It is affectionate and cute, but also aggressive and selfish. It can also be quite mischievous and has no regard for social conventions (Goldhaber & Goldhaber, 1976, p. 39). While the Natural Child is not always happy, it does not repress anything and is never indirect in expressing how it feels.

The language of the Natural Child is very simple and direct. It expresses itself with verbs such as *I want, I don't want, I like, I love, I hate, I'm happy, I'm sad, I'm mad, I'm afraid.* One version of the Natural Child particularly germane to teaching could be called the "little professor." The "little professor" writes papers and books, paints and fixes things, designs, and creates. The "little professor" enjoys participating in creative behavior and easily expresses joy (Roberts, 1975, p. 39).

There are many opportunities for the Natural Child perspective to make its own particular contribution to the experience of the teacher. Coming from a Natural Child perspective, a teacher enjoys teaching and writing and enthusiastically presents material to the students. If you have ever had the experience of teaching when creative ideas seem to come out of nowhere, you have probably experienced the Natural Child perspective. When ideas pop into your head when writing or when you feel like you are really contributing at a meeting, you also are experiencing the Natural Child perspective. When you experience the Natural Child perspective, work feels like play. The Natural Child perspective is that part of us that feels excited about learning and is thrilled with the results. Teachers can create environments for students' Natural Child perspective to emerge by showing respect for the students' ideas and feelings whatever they might be.

### Adapted Child Perspective

The Adapted Child perspective duplicates a set of the original defensive reactions the individual had toward his or her parents or chief caretakers during childhood. (Roberts, 1975, p. 13). When confronted with situations a child finds frightening, rather than dealing with the situation directly the child might adopt a coping strategy known as acting out. Acting out is characterized by inappropriate behavior or actions.

The following situations tend to evoke an Adapted Child perspective in a teacher:

1. Not knowing the answer to a question
2. Receiving some negative criticism from students
3. Being lectured to by an administrator
4. Getting pressure from a supervisor to take on a job for which you have no interest
5. Having students make too many demands on your time outside of the classroom

The following situations tend to evoke an Adapted Child perspective in students.

1. Getting graded or evaluated
2. Taking a test
3. Writing about something you don't understand
4. Receiving negative feedback on written work
5. Receiving assignments you don't understand
6. Talking to a teacher who is unsupportive of your point of view

This, then, is a brief overview of our simplified version of the transactional-analytic approach in which a teacher's internal world is composed of five perspectives: Adult, Supportive Parent, Critical Parent, Natural Child, and Adapted Child. We have found this framework useful because it provides a reasonably transparent taxonomy for talking about the different behaviors we have seen in ourselves and in our students. Moreover, as we will show, it also provides needed clarity on the complex nature of the internal world of communication. It provides a framework for making sense of what teachers observe in themselves, in other teachers, and in their students.[**]

## PREDICTING CONSEQUENCES OF THE INTERACTION BETWEEN PERSPECTIVES

One important use of the internal perspectives framework is that it can also provide a basis for understanding and managing interactions and relationships by predicting individual responses to acts of communication. We would like to explain how these predictions might work. Roberts (1975, p. 15), citing Berne (1961), characterizes two types of transactions: complementary transactions, which occur when response expectations are

---

[**]While we have adopted a fairly classical view of transactional analysis in this chapter, we introduce a modified point of view in Chapter 6.

met, and crossed transactions, which occur when response expectations are not met. Roberts describes two types of complementary transactions between Adult perspectives and between Parent and Child perspectives: Adult-Adult and Parent-Child.[6]

## Complementary Transactions

### Adult-Adult

The first type of complementary transaction is one in which both parties communicate from their Adult perspectives. For example, suppose a supervisor starts a conversation with a teacher about a proposed curriculum change. Suppose also that the supervisor starts the conversation from an Adult perspective. Knowing how she started the conversation, the supervisor would probably expect the teacher also to respond from an Adult perspective by providing additional analytic comments.

### Parent-Natural Child

The second type of complementary transaction is one in which the Parent perspective speaks to the Child perspective or the Child perspective responds to Parent perspective. For example, suppose a teacher speaks to a student from a Supportive Parent perspective by praising or encouraging the student's work. The teacher would probably expect the student to react from a Natural Child perspective by feeling and expressing pleasure, and, thus, validating the teacher's use of the Supportive Parent perspective.

## Crossed Transactions

Roberts characterizes non-complementary transactions as "crossed transactions," which are those in which response expectations are not met. In the first example, the supervisor would probably not expect the teacher to respond from the Parent perspective because this would suggest that the teacher had misinterpreted the supervisor's perspective as that of a Child and was responding accordingly. In the second example, the teacher would probably not expect the student to respond from the Parent perspective because this would suggest that the student had misinterpreted the teacher's perspective as that of a Child and was responding accordingly. Moreover, the teacher would not expect the student to respond from the Adult perspective because in doing so the student would not be validating the Supportive Parental perspective from which the teacher began the conversation.

Finally, we want to re-emphasize that "expected" responses should be used as a way of making some useful predictions about the course of communication without believing that these predictions will always be accurate. In fact, communication is certainly more complicated and involves more variables than are provided by transactional analysis (for example, see Wertsch, 1985, for an overview of Vygotskian perspectives on culture, communication, and cognition). However, we can still use the transactional analysis framework to inform our use of communication strategies to our advantage without expecting that they will work in every situation.

We believe that the goal of communication is the overall functioning of the different perspectives rather than the development of one perspective to the exclusion of the others, and we agree with Roberts that every person (including, of course, every teacher) has the capacity for fully functioning Parent, Adult, and Child perspectives (Roberts, 1975, p. 13). We also believe that there is no overall best perspective from which to respond to a situation. Each perspective has its own strengths and weaknesses, and there are no rules governing the prioritization of one perspective over the other. Each individual must make her own communication choices in order to shape, select from, or adapt to real-world environments relevant to one's life and abilities (Sternberg, 1985).

## NOTES

1. See Blackburn (1999, pp. 138–140) for a minimal definition of self as an organizing principle in which he specifically uses the term *perspective* to describe the self.

2. Some representative publications on the topic of multiple internal perspectives and evidence in support of their construct validity include Assagioli, 1972; Baker and Holden, 1976; Beahrs, 1982; Carver and Scheier, 2000; Freud, 1923/1962; Janet, 1907; Jung, 1964; Perls, 1973; White, 1980; Watkins and Johnson, 1982.

3. Freud (1923/1962, pp. 26–28, 38) proposed a controversial hypothesis that God is a psychological projection (a product of our minds). (See Vitz, 2005, for an extended discussion of this hypothesis and reactions to it). This hypothesis seems to be a version of Joseph Campbell's position when he states, "Heaven and hell are within us, and all the gods are within us. This is the great realization of the Upanishads of India in the 9th Century B.C." (Campbell, 1988, p. 39). Following Freud's line of reasoning, one might imagine that early mankind created a monotheistic deity with three aspects/faces (such as Father, Son, and Holy Spirit) in mankind's own image, and that this early tripartite view of mankind's internal world represents the same view of an internal world as does the transactional analytic framework, which we introduce on p. 46. However, it important to keep in mind that Campbell's position does not preclude the simultaneous existence of an external God as well. Moreover, using projection as support for the notion of a tripartite internal world would apply if one argues for a chain of causality starting a three-internal-perspective deity creating mankind in the deity's image. In Chapter 10, we provide a more extended discussion of projection. (See Solms, 2003, and Horgan, 1996, for current thinking on Freud's theories.)

4. Transactional analysis was first introduced to the psychological profession in Eric Bern's seminal article, "Concerning the Nature of Communication" (Berne, 1953). From here on, we will use the term *transactional analysis* to refer to *structural analysis,* a component of the general theory of transactional analysis. Structural analysis involves the recognition of an individual's ego states (i.e., multiple perspectives). While transactional analysis has undergone a great deal of popularization (Goldhaber & Goldhaber, 1976, pgs. 11–12), it is important to remember that the origins of transactional analysis are in academic research and that a great deal of empirical support exists for the theory (Baker & Holden, 1976). In addition, it has been used to organize thinking about communication with students of psychology for several decades (Ernst, 1972). The International Transactional Analysis Association *(www.itaa-net.org)* provides a wide variety of services and products, including *The Transactional Analysis Journal.*

5. Linguists over the years have proposed a variety of systems for classifying factors affecting communication events, and the systems they have come up with can be very complex. To illustrate just how complex these systems can get, we go back to Hymes's (1974) list of factors relevant to understanding how a particular communicative event achieves its objectives, including setting and scene, participants, ends, act sequence, key, instrumentalities, norms of interaction, interpretation, and genre (Hymes, as discussed in Wardhaugh, 2002, pp. 246–248). Systems such as this are very useful to linguists who have the time and expertise to develop an understanding of the components and then apply this understanding to careful scientific investigation. However, in selecting

a system for characterizing components of communication events that can be used under everyday circumstances, we need not only to be concerned with the comprehensibility and validity of the constructs involved but also with the practicality of keeping the constructs in mind and using them as the need arises. A system for organizing our thinking about communication and making deliberate decisions about how to communicate needs to be relatively compact and easy to keep in mind. For reasons we explain in Note 6, we think that transactional analysis provides just such a system.

6. According to transactional analysis, regardless of what we say, the internal perspective we happen to be in at the time of communication influences the effect of our communication on others. Moreover, the perspective that we attribute to the other person at the time of communication influences how we react to messages from others. Thus, an individual can be the source of or receive messages coming from any of the five perspectives.

> "I know you believe you understand what you think I said, but I'm not sure you realize that what you heard was not what I meant."

Ronald Adler and Neil Towne
*Looking Out, Looking In*
(1975, p. 264)

# Chapter 5

# Communication Strategies

In Chapter 4, we introduced the concept of *internal perspectives* and examined how they can affect communication in interpersonal relationships, especially with colleagues and students. In everyday communication, when we are satisfied with the results of our interactions with others, we may have little motivation for thinking about our own internal perspectives or the internal perspectives of others. However, when interpersonal communication becomes difficult, we can benefit from thinking about the effects of our internal perspectives on the outcomes of the communication. Moreover, no matter the nature of our interpersonal communications—whether our interactions go smoothly or whether we experience a few bumps—having specific communication strategies at our disposal is useful. Our ability to experience teaching as pleasure, satisfaction, or privilege depends in part on how positive and rewarding our interactions are with colleagues and students.

Chapter 5 describes three sets of communication strategies that can be used to facilitate positive interpersonal communications with students and colleagues. Strategies in the first set are designed to be used more or less independently as the need arises. We refer to this set of strategies as *listening strategies*, such as acknowledging, buying time, mirroring, rephrasing, reframing, and questioning. The second set of strategies is focused on *giving and receiving feedback*, including negative feedback. These sets of strategies are particularly useful to implement when interpersonal communications more or less take you by surprise and become unexpectedly difficult. Strategies in the third set focus on procedures for using the higher-order executive processes of reflection, goal-setting, planning, implementation, and evaluation. The strategies in the third set can be used to prepare for and carry out more lengthy, high-stakes communication tasks that involve *strategizing and problem solving.* In other words, they are useful when you have time to plan in advance. All three sets of strategies are designed to create positive experiences in communicating with others. When we learn to communicate more effectively, we gain confidence in our skills and abilities and, as a result, create more opportunities for enjoying communicating with others.

## SET 1: LISTENING STRATEGIES

Some years ago when we first started thinking seriously about improving our communication skills, especially with colleagues and students, we focused our attention primarily on learning *what* to say, thinking that if we could just be better at saying the right thing, then any problem would be solved. Perhaps we focused first on learning what to say because, like most people, we have made remarks on occasions that we later regretted or we regretted not using opportunities to say the perfect thing, hindsight being 20/20. However, soon after we began our formal study of communication strategies, we learned to our surprise that effective communication is more than learning what to say. *Effective communication* actually begins with effective listening. This does not mean that the language one uses is not important. It *is* important, and as will be shown in the strategies outlined later, we will suggest specific language for beginning to use the strategies. However, to communicate effectively, the focus must be on listening to and understanding what the other person has to say and then choosing appropriate responses.

A wide range of strategies for becoming an effective listener has been proposed in the literature (Axline, 1969; Barker, 1971; Nichols & Stevens, 1957; Rogers, 1961). Our challenge has been to reduce the number of overall strategies and to organize them into a manageable and useful set. We will introduce you to some of the listening strategies that we have found helpful. Figure 5.1 organizes these listening strategies according to the requirements needed for processing or the amount of effort required on the part of the listener. In some situations, the listener may have neither the time nor emotional stamina to think clearly about what to say. In these situations listening strategies that require less processing of information may be easier to use. For example, simply acknowledging that you have heard someone takes little effort on the part of the listener. In other situations, strategies involving more processing may prove to be more attractive, such as when the listener is invested in participating in the conversation— for example, when you want to ask the speaker a question about what she said. Figure 5.1 shows how the various strategies that we will introduce in this chapter are organized on the processing continuum.

For many of the strategies in this chapter, we will also provide examples of specific language needed to carry out the purpose of the strategy. The language one chooses to use with each of the strategies contributes to one's success in working with them. Keeping the idea of specific language

**Figure 5.1**  Strategy Processing Requirements

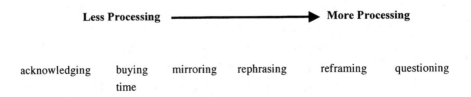

in mind, we suggest memorizing specific language (i.e., phrases and sentences) for working with each of the strategies. Memorizing language can be important when using the strategies is new and unfamiliar because if you're thinking about what you should say, you cannot listen effectively.

### Acknowledging

The most neutral form of listening is a simple *acknowledgment*, which consists of letting the speaker know that he or she has been heard. Some commonly used acknowledgments follow. In each example, the listener refers to you and the speaker refers to whomever you are talking to—e.g., a student, a colleague, a supervisor.

*Listener:*    (nods in agreement)

*Listener:*    "I hear you."

*Listener:*    Hmmm. . . .

*Listener:*    "That makes perfect sense."

*Listener:*    "Thanks for telling me about this."

*Listener:*    uh huh. . . .

Acknowledgments when sincerely offered are effective in avoiding the Critical Parent or Adapted Child's perspectives. The acknowledging strategy can also serve as a transition to the next strategy, buying time.

### Buying Time

*Buying time* consists of letting the speaker know you realize that the issue or the problem is an important one, that you would like to have some time to think about it before responding, and that you would like to discuss the situation at a specific time in the future. Buying time is useful when you genuinely need more thinking time to generate a considered response or when the communication is confrontational. The following are examples of strategies for buying time:

*Listener:* "I want you to know that I hear everything you said, and I want to consider it carefully. Can you let me have some time to think about it and get back to you within _____ ." (*Insert time period such as a couple of hours, days, etc.*)

*Listener:* "I'd like just a little time to think about what you said before I respond. Okay?"

If the communication occurs in public and is somewhat confrontational, this language is useful:

*Listener:* "I want you to know that I heard what you said, but I'd like to talk to you further in private. Okay?"

## Mirroring

Another effective listening strategy is called *mirroring*. In mirroring the listener tries to slow down the conversation so that he or she can repeat what the speaker said. The only change the listener makes is to change the pronouns as needed in the context (Hendrix, 1992). Optionally, the listener can then check to see whether he or she has repeated the message accurately and/or ask if there is more. Checking for accuracy shows that the listener cares about the details of the speaker's message. Asking the speaker if there is more he or she wants to say shows that the listener intends to continue listening until the speaker has said everything. This strategy provides additional validation of the speaker's feelings and point of view.

This example illustrates the mirroring strategy:

*Speaker:* "I've been really upset about the grade you gave me on my last paper, and. . ., and. . ., and. . . ."

*Listener:* "Do you mind if I slow our conversation down a little so that I can make certain I've heard your concerns correctly? I think you said that you've been really upset about the grade that I gave you on your last paper. Is that right? (Wait for speaker to acknowledge that you have heard him or her correctly.) Is there more?"

Before using the mirroring strategy with others, you might want to ask for permission, as shown in this example:

*Speaker:* "I've been really upset with you recently, and. . ., and. . ., and. . ."

*Listener:* "I really want to make certain that I understand your concerns. I can understand your concerns better if you will allow me listen to what you have to say one piece at a time and then rephrase it to see if I have heard you correctly. Would you be willing to try this with me?"

Although this strategy appears simple, there are several reasons why it can actually be somewhat difficult to do well. First, if you are executing this strategy correctly, you cannot say just anything that pops into your mind at any time. Second, it requires that you truly listen to the details of what the other person is saying. Third, it is often difficult to simply repeat information with a neutral tone and without judgment or sarcasm. This may be especially true on those occasions when the language is emotionally charged and some of the negative emotions are directed at you. Mirroring is also very effective in trying to help students who may be struggling with clarity in their thinking.

### Rephrasing

*Rephrasing* involves restating or summarizing the content of the message in different words without adding or subtracting any important content. Using this strategy allows the speaker to talk for a couple of minutes at a time instead of saying just one or two sentences at a time as in mirroring. As with mirroring, you may want to ask permission first (see the example language on page 61). Here is an example of rephrasing:

> *Speaker:* "I don't understand why I got the grade I did on this es say. You haven't written very many comments so I'm confused. I don't really know what you expect from us. Why did I get a 'C'? You give us assignments, we do them, and then you grade the assignments on things you never tell us about."
>
> *Listener:* "So, let me see if I understand. I think you said that you don't understand why you got the grade you did and that you think I don't provide you with enough information about how I grade. Is that right?"

Many teachers find rephrasing more conversationally comfortable because the communication sounds more natural than mirroring. However, rephrasing is more difficult than mirroring in several ways. First, it requires that you keep more detailed information in mind before responding. Second, it requires that you think about what you are saying and work creatively to change the form but not the content. Third, it requires that in this creative process you do not allow yourself to add your own opinions. *This point is very important!* If you watch highly effective interviewers in the media, you will see them use this strategy because it indicates to the person being interviewed that the interviewer is genuinely paying attention to and interested in what the interviewee has to say.[1]

People who are very good at rephrasing are often able to break the speaker's message down into two parts: one part of the message responds to the speaker's internal world (particularly his or her feelings), and one part of the message responds to the details of the speaker's external world. For example, consider the following:

> *Speaker:* "You only criticize my writing and point out my mistakes. I don't think you like anything I say."
>
> *Listener:* "It sounds like you feel bad when I make a lot of comments and marks on your paper. Is that right?"

Starting the rephrasing with "it sounds like" helps the listener come across as less intrusive because it indicates that the listener is reporting on his or her understanding of what was said instead of assuming he or she knows exactly how the speaker feels. While rephrasing is more conversationally natural than mirroring, there are some drawbacks. It is important to be aware that some speakers may feel like the words they use are exactly what they mean, and they may they object to any changes the listeners might make in how their meaning is expressed. If this is the case, you can always try mirroring (i.e., restating the exact words).

### Reframing

*Reframing* provides a different context for a message, a context that is frequently used to change the focus of a message from negative to positive.[2] "Reframing. . . .make(s) statements of responsibility that empower (one's) choice in a situation, rather than being a victim"[3] (Shepherd, 2007).

One straightforward way to word a reframe is to change the language of the message from "don't want" to "want" or "do want."[4] This reframe is worded in the language of the Natural Child perspective (associated with feeling and wanting) and is intended to evoke the Natural Child state of mind. An example of how a teacher might reframe a student's complaint follows.

> *Speaker:* "These instructions are confusing us. We've read the instructions several times, but we're so confused. We can't figure out what you want us to do." (The "don't want" component of the student's message is that the students don't want to be confused.)
>
> *Listener:* "It sounds like you want the instructions to be as clear as possible so you can do your best."

The graphic shows a new (positive) frame around the original statement.

Using the strategies of mirroring, rephrasing, and reframing with non-native speakers, such as ESL learners, requires an additional level of expertise on the part of the listener. It is important for the listener to use appropriate L2 teacher talk (e.g., slow down, pause frequently, simplify the

**Figure 5.2**    Positive Frame of Original Statements

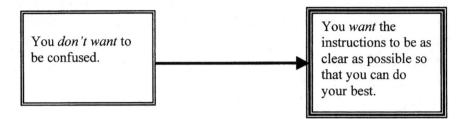

syntax, rephrase, and repeat). In addition, it is also important to carefully consider the level of proficiency of the language learner and take into consideration such things as the learner's limited knowledge of syntax, ability to use a wide range of appropriate vocabulary items, control of register, etc. Experienced L2 teachers are often quite good at this, but we have found that it is useful to clarify if there is any doubt. (e.g., *Do you mean? Let me see if I understood you correctly*). The focus for the listener is on the propositions in the message, not the exact language the speaker may use. If you are hesitant to use these strategies with language learners, it might be useful for you to know that we have used all three strategies with L2 learners with success both in terms of the outcome of the communication and the feedback we have received from the learners themselves.

### Effect on the Speaker (the Person Whose Message Has Been Reframed)

For the speaker whose message has been reframed by a listener, the reframe provides reassurance that the speaker has been heard. It also provides evidence that the listener has paid enough attention to the speaker's message to have considered its content and implications (the implications consisting of the positive spin put on the message). This process prepares the speaker to pay attention to what the listener might add to the conversation when it becomes the listener's turn to speak.

### Reframings Effect on the Listener (the Person Doing the Reframing)

For the listener, the reframe provides a potential for switching perspectives—i.e., from a person who might be defensive (the Adapted Child perspective) to one who may be encouraging (the Supportive Parent perspective speaking deliberately in language that that Natural Child perspective can relate to). In doing so, it puts the listener on the same side as the speaker. In addition, reframing helps the listener avoid emotional hijacking when preparing to talk with someone with whom the listener is upset; this is illustrated under Sequencing (below). Once this shift of perspective has taken place, whatever additional information the speaker may provide about the listener's complaint is more likely to come from the Supportive Parent perspective and, thus, is more likely to be heard.

## Reframing Self-Judgments

Reframing is not only a useful strategy for communicating with others; it can also be used to frame judgments about ourselves in a more positive context. When we judge ourselves, there is no external individual situation that we can hold accountable for our failures, or nothing that we can try to change. Thus, we need a strategy that is entirely internal, such as reframing. For example, if you are mad at someone else, you can think there is a chance that the other person will change. But if you are mad at yourself, it is clear that the problem is entirely within you, and changing yourself is the only logical solution. This dialogue is an example of a reframe of a self-judgment.

| | |
|---|---|
| *Teacher's self-judgment:* | "I should have known the answer to that student's questions. I didn't prepare enough. I'm lazy." |
| *Teacher's reframe:* | "I always want to be prepared. I want to do the best possible job." |

Experienced teachers know that part of learning how to teach effectively is learning how to reflect critically on one's teaching. For some teachers, the balance between critical reflection and self-judgment is difficult to find, and there are always some teachers who tend to judge their work too harshly, particularly new teachers. New teachers may not have enough experience with teaching to realize that teaching is a variable process and that ups and downs are natural. It is possible to help teachers reframe self-judgments and in doing so further their abilities to reflect critically on their own work.

Although we have had many positive experiences with the listening strategy of reframing and have found it very useful, we would like to point out that it is subject to the same limitations as rephrasing: Some speakers prefer their exact words rather than any interpretation of their words. Moreover, by virtue of the fact that reframing relies on a formula, its overuse can come across as mechanical if the listener is not constantly monitoring for the possibility.

Our experience with the effects of reframing over the long term are that reframing one's judgments of oneself and others can play a significant role in one's own internal transformation, similar to the role that sustained and supportive communication can play in helping another person develop self-confidence and a positive self-image.[5]

## Reframing Feedback to Students

Another use of reframing is turning constructive feedback (often deemed by students to be negative feedback) into positive statements. An actual example of this came up for us recently when a beginning ESL writing teacher knew that a student had plagiarized a paper (a good portion of the final essay was unlike anything the student had ever produced or seemed capable of producing). This new teacher was so worried that the student might react defensively that she seemed almost incapable of bringing up the subject with him. We suggested that the teacher reframe her negative opinion of the student's work as follows:

**Figure 5.3**    Negative Opinion Reframe

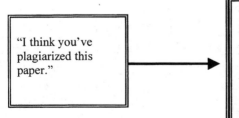

## Questioning

Another effective listening strategy that we have found very useful is *questioning*, which consists of eliciting additional specific information about a speaker's experience. It can have the effect of helping the listener personalize his or her participation and becoming actively involved in the speaker's experience. Since questioning is designed to get the speaker talking, it is best to avoid yes/no questions that can be answered in a single word. In addition, our experience has also shown us that it is helpful to be knowledgeable about possible negative consequences of the use of questions:

> Asking questions can be very counterproductive although many people think they are trying to show interest when asking questions. However, asking questions can have the opposite effect, as some people feel attacked when several questions are asked. This can be especially true when they're asked numerous questions in succession. (Brown, 2001, p.163–164)

Therefore, if you ask questions, it is important to demonstrate a genuine curiosity and interest in the answers. Focus carefully on each question, use indirect questioning techniques, and try not to rush the process. For the purpose of manageability, we have grouped questions into the following three categories.

### Wh- Detail Questions

*Wh-* detail questions are typically formed with a *wh-* word as the focus, such as *where, when,* or *what,* (and *how*) and are used to elicit specific, limited facts about the speaker's experience. They show additional interest on the part of the listener. These questions typically do not require analysis on the part of the listener and can be answered quite briefly, and they tend to be the least personal category of questions. We have found that *wh-* questions can be quite useful in helping the speaker feel comfortable about talking. Softening the questions with introductory phrases, such as *Do you remember. . ., Do you know. . .,* or *Can you tell me. . .* (i.e., making indirect questions) is helpful, especially if you intend to ask several questions in a row.

### Tell Me About Questions

Although not technically questions, we call them *tell me about* questions because their purpose is to elicit responses, similar to questions. *Tell me about* questions are general in nature and designed let the speaker talk about whatever seems to be significant in his or her experience. Some examples of general questions are:

To a colleague who seems to be upset: "I'd really like you to tell me about what's upset you."

To a student who is upset about a course grade: "I'd be very interested in knowing what a course grade means to you."

To a supervisor who seems to have difficulty with your style of working: "I'd like you to tell me about what your experience is of supervising me on the job."

### Analysis Questions

Analysis questions require the speaker to reflect on and organize his or her thoughts about an experience in particular ways. These questions can be classified into categories that correspond to the kinds of rhetorical organizational structures commonly taught in writing classes (see McCrimmon, 1984; Hunt, 1984). Notice that some of the questions are stated as directives rather than syntactic questions and that all of the questions need softening phrases, such as those previously mentioned in *wh-* detail and *Tell me about* questions (e.g., What were the most and least useful parts of this assignment? versus Do you think you could tell me what the most and least useful parts of this assignment were?) However, in order to keep the focus of the example questions that follow on the analysis features (e.g., comparison, contrast, cause/effect, etc.), we have not supplied the softening language here.

*Speaker:*    "I'm having trouble with this assignment."

*Listener:*    (Comparison): "In what ways were your reactions to this assignment similar to your reactions to previous assignments?"

(Contrast): "In what ways are the requirements of this assignment different from the requirements of other assignments that have seemed more doable?"

(Cause-effect): "What have you learned, if anything, from doing this assignment? What effects do you think that doing this assignment might have on your writing?"

(Causal analysis): "What was the chain of events that lead to your deciding not to finish the assignment? How did each event lead to the next?"

(Argumentation): "What arguments could you come up with for not including an assignment such as this in the course?"

(Analysis) "In what ways do the different parts of this assignment evoke different reactions on your part?"

(Narration): "Could you take me through steps in the process you went through in trying to do this assignment?"

(Description): "Could you describe some of the circumstances in your life that are relevant to your reaction to this assignment?"

Listening plays a pivotal role in communication and in developing rewarding and meaningful interpersonal relationships. While it may take some practice and commitment to become familiar with the listening strategies described, the practice is worth the effort. With a bit of practice the strategies can become second nature to you so that communication with students and colleagues will feel respectful and rewarding regardless of whether or not you agree with their points of view.

## SET 2: STRATEGIES FOR GIVING AND RECEIVING FEEDBACK

All teachers give or receive feedback at one time or another. The strategies that follow are designed to make the process of giving and receiving feedback as productive and positive as possible. Giving and receiving negative feedback is never easy, but there are ways to structure the feedback that make it better for all persons involved in the interaction. The examples that follow may focus on giving and receiving negative feedback because negative experiences can prevent us from getting at the heart of our own teaching and from the ability to experience teaching from a positive viewpoint, as an experience of pleasure, satisfaction, or privilege. If you often enjoy positive experiences in your teaching and in your communication with your students and colleagues, no doubt your communication strategies are working well for you. Nevertheless, we believe that everyone can benefit from having conscious knowledge of how to use specific strategies in communication when and if difficulties arise.

### Strategies for Giving Feedback (as a Speaker)

### Orient Yourself

If the feedback you must give is somewhat negative, try not to dwell on the negativity of your feedback. Focusing on the negative may put you into a Critical Parent perspective, and if you communicate from this perspective, you are likely to elicit a defensive (Adapted Child) response from the listener. In such circumstances, it is useful to take some time to redirect the focus of attention away from the negative feedback itself. You can do this by focusing your attention on the person receiving the feedback and imagining that the listener is totally open to and positive about communicating with you.* In this state of mind, decide what you want to say. If you succeed in accomplishing this, you are more likely to provide feedback from an Adult perspective, making statements of fact with no judgments.

### Ask for Permission

Asking for permission involves letting the listener know that you would like to provide some feedback and asking whether the listener would be willing to receive this feedback. This process allows the listener the opportunity to participate in setting the context for the conversation and tends to engage the Supportive Parent perspective.

---

*A wide variety of specific procedures for doing this can be found in Bandler, Grinder, and Connirea (1989).

### Begin with Strengths

Beginning with strengths involves looking for what the listener is good at and acknowledging these strengths before you talk about things that need improvement. Beginning with strengths engages the Supportive Parent perspective and helps the listener feel more relaxed and open (Westberg & Hilliard, 1994).

### *Strategies for Receiving Feedback (as a Listener)*

For many teachers interpersonal communication that is somewhat negative is frightening. It never feels good to be criticized or to have someone be upset in your presence. A general strategy for creating safety for yourself in such situations is to try to take some control of the situation so you have some say in what happens and know what to expect. Simple procedures like telling yourself you will only listen to the feedback without conveying any negative reaction verbally or nonverbally can help to give you some space. For example, you can make an agreement with yourself that you will only listen and will not respond substantively for 24 hours or until you are not feeling reactive.

### Seek to Understand and Focus on Solution

In situations where there is a problem and individuals are angry and upset with you, as difficult as it might be, it is important to seek to understand the problem by using the listening and questioning strategies given previously. Try to ignore personal attacks for the time being and focus on generating solutions to the problem. Keep asking how you can help solve the problem. Also, try, if possible, to avoid criticizing anyone else or anyone else's individual response. Try not to take the situation personally.

### Select a Messenger Whom You Trust

One common situation that almost every teacher finds difficult is receiving negative course evaluations. Part of what makes this difficult is that the evaluations are typically anonymous, so there is no friendly face with whom to associate the feedback. As a result, it is easy to imagine that the critical comments are coming from one's most negative student. A way to soften the effect of the criticism is to find a colleague whom you trust and who is supportive to help you. Ask your colleague to read your evaluations and rephrase the negative feedback to be as constructive as possible or to rephrase the negative feedback to focus on solutions. Also, ask your colleague to balance the negative feedback with the positive feedback so that you balance your own thinking. If your colleague speaks from a Supportive Parent perspective, this will tend to elicit a response from your Natural Child perspective in which you take responsibility for improving your teaching without getting defensive.

The communicative strategies described are not meant to be exhaustive. They are simply examples of the types of skills that you can develop in order to improve interpersonal communication so that you can experience your interpersonal relationships as pleasure, satisfaction, or privilege. With practice the strategies can be internalized to the point that they can be used naturally and easily as needs arise.

## SET 3: USING THE EXECUTIVE PROCESSES TO ORGANIZE AND SEQUENCE COMMUNICATION STRATEGIES

While the communication strategies previously described are useful individually in their own right, they can be even more useful when you can plan for the communication and integrate the strategies into a careful process. Chapter 1 introduced the higher-order executive processes of reflection, goal setting, planning, implementation, and evaluation. Using these executive processes to organize and sequence communication can be especially helpful in avoiding the negative effects of emotional hijacking in situations in which you know your communication is likely to be driven by your emotions. Such situations might include having to announce a controversial decision, speak to parents of a student who is doing poorly in your class, or deal with a supervisor who is upset with you or with whom you are upset.

### 1. Reflection

The purpose of reflection is to think about the problem or situation and make a commitment to using the executive process to develop a logical plan carrying out communication. We have found it useful to begin this process by implementing the buying time strategy. In buying time, you ask to make an appointment to discuss the issues. The distance you are able to create with this strategy will give you time to focus on the executive processes and provide you with clarity about the issues before you engage in communication.

## *2. Goal Setting*

Goal setting involves establishing in your own mind the characteristics of the process and, possibly, the outcome of the communication. Some basic goals that we have found provide a constructive context for communication are:

a. Commit to an informed process in which you do your best to remain open to a variety of outcomes, depending upon the information that comes out in the communication.

b. Commit to maintaining your respect for an individual's right to his or her opinion and/or position, regardless of whether or not you agree with each other.

c. Commit to an opportunity for each person to ask completely for what he or she wants and to be acknowledged.

d. Commit to communicating from the perspective(s) from which you want to come during the communication (such as the Adult or Supportive Parent perspectives).

## *3. Planning*

Planning involves breaking down a communication event into a sequence of events and practicing specific communication strategies you might use in each stage. A logical, general sequence of events that we have used with success follows.

## a. Let the other person clear the air about the past.

Invite the other individual to express his or her position and listen until the person is complete. Select from the listening strategies covered in this chapter and listen actively until the other person is complete. Do your best to put yourself in the other person's position and see the positive intention** behind his or her behavior.

## b. Clear the air about your own experience.

After you have established that the other person feels complete with describing his or her experience, describe your own experience. Preface your description with a statement to the effect that you are not asking the other person to agree with you but just to hear what you have to say. Avoid either minimizing or exaggerating the description of your feelings.

## c. Have each person ask completely for what he or she wants.

Invite the other person to ask for what he or she wants in the best of all possible worlds, with no compromises. Actively listen to the other person's request. Then ask for exactly what you want. Express what you want as a position, not an ultimatum. Do not compromise in what you ask for at this point. It is important that each person involved in the interaction understand what the other wants.

## d. Generate a set of possible solutions and negotiate.[6]

Generate a possible set of options and focus on the positive intentions behind what you and the other person want. Both parties must accept the fact that neither party may get exactly what he or she wants.

### 4. Implementation

Implementation involves carrying out your prearranged plan. One way to start is to explain to the individual that you would like to talk in

---

**The term *positive intention* is also used in Bandler & Grinder, 1982, p. 114.

such a way to make sure that both parties understand each other. In order to do this, you will need to take turns speaking until each of you feels like you have said everything you need to say. Ask the individual if this would be all right with him or her.

Once you have thought through each stage, take some time to practice specific communication strategies that will keep you on track during your communication. You may want to keep a notecard with you that lists the specific strategies you have planned to use. You can pause during the communication and use your notes.

## 5. Evaluation

Evaluation includes carefully looking at the characteristics of both the internal and external worlds after the communication has occurred. In difficult situations, we typically focus on just a few external facts, but we have a large number of thoughts, feelings, ideas, stories, explanations, and justifications that constitute our internal reaction to these few external facts. However, internal reactions to facts are highly variable both between individuals and within any single individual. For example, one individual may react to a situation as being humorous while another individual may react to the same situation as disturbing. Moreover, a single individual may react to the same set of events (such as the events of one's childhood) very differently at different times in one's life.[7] In addition, the propensity of different individuals to select different facts as relevant to any event provides even more evidence of the subjective basis of our internal experience.*** When we take responsibility for our internal experiences, we simply acknowledge that the cause of our internal experiences is due in large part to this internal variability and not only to external events or to the behaviors of other individuals.[8] Evaluation helps us see the truth in this statement, and seeing the truth in this statement, and embracing the reality of it are the catalysts for creating experiences of pleasure, satisfaction, or privilege.

---

***See Blackburn (1999), Chapter 7, for a discussion of relativism.

### Evaluation of External Facts

We have found it helpful to begin the process of evaluation by listing the external facts involved in a given experience. We do this in order to help us understand how we participate in creating our own reality. If you have never done this before, we think you may be surprised to learn that the facts are so few. Answer the *wh-* questions about external factors: *what, who, where, when, how,* etc. (<u>Note</u>: do not use *why* in this reflection.)

### Evaluation of Your Internal Response to External Facts

After making a list of who did what, when, and where, write down your reactions to the situation. The length of your list will vary, depending on the strength of your feelings about the experience. Think about the relationship between the two lists. How many of your reactions are about who? When? What?

### Evaluation of the Underlying Causes of Internal Responses

A formula we have found useful in getting at the underlying causes of our internal responses is to determine what you want from the experience, what you feel you deserve or are entitled to, and what you actually got (Keys, 1975; Richo, 1993, pp. 5–6). For example, let's suppose that one of your professional goals as a teacher is to improve the quality of the alternative assessment instruments you use in your classes. You have worked hard to develop several alternative assessments for your students, avoiding traditional tests altogether and allowing students opportunities to select which alternative assessment best fits their learning styles and gives them the opportunity to show what they have learned. Several students do poorly despite your efforts and are upset as a result. Their behavior is somewhat aggressive and negative toward you and the class. You find yourself feeling angry with these students. Understanding the underlying cause of your anger may be useful in helping you respond appropriately to the students. Using the formula provided, start by determining exactly what you want, what you feel you deserve, and what you did not get. For example, you might have wanted all of your students to recognize how hard you worked at creating the alternative assessments. You might also have wanted your students to recognize how much you cared about them and cared about giving them opportunities to do their best. You might also feel that you deserve this recognition since you worked so hard and had your students' interests and welfare at heart. In addition, you can clearly see that you did not get what you wanted and felt you deserved.

It is certainly not our intention to trivialize the challenge of letting go of what we feel we deserve or the dangers of denying feelings or trying to talk ourselves into believing we don't want something that we do. Instead, we offer the strategy for analyzing the cause of our internal reactions as a psychological tool to help put the focus of the problem and the responsibility for doing something about it on ourselves, a process that keeps us from feeling like victims. Taking responsibility gives us a feeling of hope for a resolution, even if the resolution is in the long term. Moreover, trusting in long-term solutions helps us avoid desperately seeking or demanding short-term solutions when they may not be possible.[9] For example, instead of focusing on the short-term goal of creating effective alternative assessment measures for our current students, we may switch to creating effective alternative assessment over the long term, thereby seeing each attempt along the way, whether successful or unsuccessful, as a step toward our ultimate goal. Switching to long-term goals helps us focus on changes in our own internal world, so that situations that would previously have upset us no longer do so.

### Evaluation of Another Person's Positive Traits

Taking stock of another individual's positive traits is useful in providing some balance for negative feelings that often arise in emotionally charged communication. You might find some of these activities useful.

a. Make a list of the individual's strengths, including specific qualities of the individual that you value, regardless of the difficulties you may be having with the individual at the moment.
b. Identify characteristics of the individual that are obviously different from yours and list ways in which people with these characteristics enrich your experience of diversity.

c. Imagine that whatever the individual is doing is being done innocently, without any malice directed toward you. List some reasons for the person's behavior that have nothing to do with you. (This tends to depersonalize the situation.)

Using some of the evaluation strategies described can help us get a sense of perspective and start to establish a more balanced view of the problematic circumstances.

Although we have spent considerable time focusing on the difficulties associated with interpersonal communication, we do not want to give the impression that we view teachers' lives in general as filled with one difficult communicative encounter after another or that the strategies we suggest are useful only when communication becomes difficult. Clearly this is not the case. In fact, most teachers' lives are full of many successful and positive interactions. However, we believe that it is the difficult interactions that can keep us from experiencing teaching as pleasurable, satisfying, or a privilege and, ultimately, keep us from the heart of teaching. When communication is going well, we do not think much about the strategies that we need for effective communication. But, the fact of the matter is that these strategies are useful in all interpersonal communications, not just the encounters that are difficult. Having a conscious understanding of the strategies we need for effective communication can serve us well in all walks of life. If we do not have the strategies for dealing with difficult communication events, we will be unable to enjoy the positive experiences that are available to us.

## NOTES

1. For example, popular U.S. radio and television sports commentator Jim Rome frequently employs rephrasing when interviewing guests on his shows. So do many other interviewers.

2. Bateson (1972) provided us with our earliest introduction to the topic of reframing (see also Watzlawick, 1978). Psychologists Erikson and Satir developed therapeutic approaches involving the use of reframing. For an account of Erikson's work, see Hayley (1993). For an account of Satir's work, see Andreas (1999). In popular literature written for the general public, Bandler and Grinder (1982),

Bandler, Grinder, and Connirea (1989), and Robbins (1986, pp. 253–272) provide a wide range of techniques for reframing that go far beyond the very limited linguistic strategy described here. A general-purpose, six-step process for reframing can be found in Bandler and Grinder (1979, p. 160). Publications dealing with positive thinking, an essential component of reframing, include the numerous works of authors such as Dale Carnegie (1981), Napoleon Hill (1987), Norman Vincent Peale (1956), and W. Clement Stone (1962).

3. Refer to Shepherd (2007) and McKay, Davis, and Fanning (1981) for a general treatment of the topic of reframing, which they refer to as self-talk. Lakoff (2004) provides a more specific treatment of the role of reframing in debate.

4. The specific "don't want → want" and "don't want → do want" reframes seem to be the most general purpose and widely used of all reframes. An Internet search yielded many hundreds of hits on organizations and programs advocating the use of these specific reframes, as well as discussions of possible reasons for their effectiveness (see Critzer, 2001). Robbins (2004) uses this reframe in his work, because he has found that "If you focus on what you want, you move toward it." In motorcycle rider training courses, riders are taught this same principle. In the event of a possible collision, they are instructed to look where they want to go to avoid the accident rather than at the location of the potential collision because the motorcycle will tend to go in the direction of the rider's focus of attention.

5. For a description of a highly structured, extended practice in reframing judgments, see Katie (2000).

6. For example, see Fisher, Ury, and Patton (1991) and Cowan, Palomares, and Schilling (1992) for an in-depth description of the negotiation process.

7. In fact, one of the goals of "personal growth" or "inner work" can be to change the nature of one's experience of one's childhood, for example, from one of victimhood to responsibility.

8. In some circles, the idea of "taking responsibility" is taken far beyond what we are describing (i.e., responsibility for our experience of events). For example, in such circles, taking responsibility is extended to events in the external world that impact us, or even all events in the external world, or even the very existence of the external world itself. We think it is important to keep the distinction between our limited interpretation and the expanded interpretation clearly in mind. (See Chapter 2, Figure 2.1, for a visual representation of what we think it is reasonable to take responsibility for, namely, the contribution of the internal signals.)

9. If you are upset by something someone did, you add to that by getting upset that you cannot find a quick way to put an end to your feeling upset. In the short term, just feeling upset without doing anything to make things worse might be just about the only thing you can do.

> "The best teachers I know are aware of their strengths and are actively involved in the process of becoming better teachers."

Linda Shalaway
*Learning to Teach*
(1989, p. 263)

# Chapter 6

# Teacher Specialties

$A$s teachers we all have special ways of presenting ourselves in the classroom. We may be shy, gregarious, helpful, easygoing, difficult, serious, or light hearted. The way we present ourselves in the classroom or the way we come across to our students is our teaching personality (Fairhurst & Fairhurst, 1995). Regardless of the type of teaching personality we have, it is important that we be aware of it. While we believe that no one teaching personality is inherently more successful than another, we maintain that it is the degree to which we are aware of our teaching personality and the effect it has on our students and colleagues that determine how successful we are in using our teaching personality to further our teaching.

This chapter addresses the issue of teaching personalities by introducing the concept of a teaching specialty. We define *specialty* as a specific set of behaviors associated with a particular internal perspective. Specialties are behaviors that we have mastered and do extremely well. We may not be aware of these behaviors or specialties, so we tend to overuse them in situations where we feel unsure of ourselves, unsafe, or threatened in some way.[1] In addition, and more important, we often overuse specialties because they have become entrenched in our behavior as habits. We often automatically use a specialty to get through a difficult situation.

Before we examine specialties in detail, let us talk about the concept in general so that it will make more sense to you. A specialty that you might recognize by name without a great deal of explanation is called *Analytic*. (From here on, we will capitalize specialties and put them in italics to distinguish them from internal perspectives and ordinary adjectives.) The strength of a person with the *Analytic* specialty is, of course, the person's analytic ability: The person is good at analyzing and providing structure for information. However, this specialty can sometimes be used as a defense in situations where the individual may feel insecure, such as during the first day of class. In such an environment, the specialty *Analytic* may manifest itself as analyzing things too much and explaining this analysis to others (i.e., talking too much out of the fear that if I don't let my students know how much I know and how smart I am, I'll appear stupid).

An obvious question to ask about teaching specialties is, "How many specialties are there?" While making a list of specialties can be interesting, such a list can end up not being very useful if it grows into a long, unorganized collection of names identifying an ever-expanding variety of behaviors. We realized that if we were to better understand teaching specialties and their importance in developing ourselves as teachers and in experiencing teaching as pleasurable, satisfying, or as a privilege, we needed a system to identify, categorize, and work with the different teaching specialties that we observe.[2]

This chapter will consider specialties within the internal perspectives framework presented in Chapter 3 that provides us with a manageable system within which to consider teacher specialties.

## GENERAL TYPES OF SPECIALTIES

In our interpretation of transactional analysis, we use five internal perspectives, and we will use these internal perspectives as a starting point for classifying specialties. As you recall from our discussion of classical transactional analysis in Chapter 4, two of the perspectives (e.g., Adapted Child and Critical Parent) are negative in nature. While we still find the interpretation of the transactional model presented in Chapter 4 useful when talking about communication principles, we wanted to avoid the negative connotations associated with the Critical Parent and Natural Child perspectives when using the perspectives to talk about specialties. Consequently, we will try to refer to all of the specialties, including those associated with the Critical Parent and Adapted Child perspectives, in terms of the *strengths* inherent in the perspective. For example, with the *Analytic* specialty, the strength, obviously, is the ability to analyze. In addition, we also look at the specialty in overuse. For example, when the specialty *Analytic* is overused, the individual may be so focused on analyzing things that he or she may appear robotic or emotionless. In a school setting, the analytic strength is useful in organizing and planning lessons and in responding to student work, but it may not be effective as a response to a colleague who is distressed over a policy that resulted in the loss of his job. When specialties are overused, teachers are unable to use the higher-order executive processes of reflection, goal-setting, planning, implementation, and evaluation. The consequences of overuse can be negative, but the underlying strength in the specialty is always positive.

With these considerations in mind, we present the following taxonomy for categorizing and classifying specialties. We frame each specialty in a positive way so that teachers are reminded that specialties are really strengths.

| Perspective | Specialty (i.e., the strength) | Specialty in overuse |
|---|---|---|
| Adult | *Analytic* | emotionless |
| Supportive Parent | *Helpful* | exhausted |
| Critical Parent | *Influential* | judgmental |
| Natural Child | *Playful* | performer |
| Adapted Child | *Sensitive* | victim |

A variety of different behaviors or "flavors" are associated with the overuse of specialties. For example, the specialty *Helpful* in overuse may come across as exhausted because this individual is helping others all of the time.

The effects of specialties permeate teaching and can either work to the teacher's advantage or disadvantage. The positive effect of being aware of a teaching specialty (and using it appropriately) is that this awareness can bring about a global shift in effectiveness and satisfaction. The negative effect is that not being aware of the specialty and using it inappropriately can impose a limit on levels of effectiveness and satisfaction that are attainable.

To help you understand more about specialties and how they work, we will describe one specialty in detail. Then, we will provide capsule descriptions of the different specialties presented. Then we will identify several specific steps we might take to work with specialties in order to become more effective teachers.[3]

## SPECIALTY EXAMPLE: *HELPFUL*

Since teaching is in many ways about helping others, it is not surprising that many teachers have the specialty *Helpful,* a specialty associated with the Supportive Parent perspective.

Teacher A is noted among her peers for being very busy with a variety of projects. A brief summary of the extraordinary range of activities she was involved in during a particular week in which we observed and interviewed her includes:

- She volunteered to put together a final exam for the class she was teaching to be used by a number of other teachers teaching different sections of the same class.
- She volunteered to organize a picnic for teachers and students in the department.
- She cooked for the picnic, prepared a master syllabus for her fellow teaching assistants, and developed a filing system for teaching resources for the department.

All of these projects were job related and important in improving the quality of the program, but they were voluntary and definitely fell outside of her job description.

During our interview with Teacher A, she told us she realized that she was overextended (quite the understatement!). She also said that she was afraid if she didn't help out, she would look cold and uncaring to others. She indicated that she frequently found herself facing two uncomfortable choices: (1) taking on tasks she knew she didn't really have time for and exhausting herself in the process or (2) refusing to help and feeling heartless and uncaring. Because the second choice was even more uncomfortable for her than the first, she often got involved in things that she later regretted. Teacher A rarely just sat around doing nothing, but she told us that she often wished she did. In addition to her volunteer work on the job, she traveled back and forth between home and work several times each day for a variety of reasons—forgotten papers, checking on sick animals, running errands for her husband—and all of these activities added to her busyness. She knew that she had trouble slowing down and taking time for herself, and she said she frequently felt exhausted, haggard, and burned out.

We also talked with her about the effect of her specialty on her teaching. She recognized that she often took on so many projects and activities she compromised the quality of work she did as a graduate student and the quality of her course preparation as a teacher. She often stayed up late at night, sacrificing her health and sleep in order to maintain her involvement in these activities. She said the overuse of her specialty also caused problems because she was afraid to give low grades, and she often spent so much time helping students that she almost did the work for them rather than letting them take responsibility for it. In her words, "I hate for people to feel uncomfortable around me. I felt like this yesterday with a student who didn't seem to know the purpose of my class. The more off track she gets, the more I try to help her out. I'm finding that I have no time for myself."

As teaching supervisors, we observed Teacher A's specialty in action and have, at various times, contributed to her busy life; we realized that we often approach her first when we need to get something done. In fact, we almost automatically ask her for help since, on some level, we must know that she is the least likely person to say no. However, we have also sensed that she frequently agrees to do what we ask even though her heart isn't really into the project. Based on this experience with Teacher A, we have agreed to consider these factors in working with teachers and students with the *Helpful* specialty.[4]

Becoming aware of and responding differently to one's specialty is not an easy task because of the relationship between one's specialty to one's individuality. In Teacher A's case, on the one hand, being helpful contributed to her individuality in that it distinguished her from other teaching assistants with different specialties. However, her helpfulness as an overused habitual way of behaving also detracted from her individuality by presenting her as one-dimensional and predictable, yet we know from talking with Teacher A that she had a wider range of potential thoughts, feelings, and behaviors than she generally exhibited. Indeed, these potentially different ways of behaving frequently went unexpressed, so, in a way, the full richness of who she was went unnoticed because of her overuse of her specialty. A specialty in overuse, therefore, has the potential to limit the range of expression we have and our individuality.

## A VARIETY OF SPECIALTIES

To help us understand the different specialties, we need to elaborate on the characteristics of the behaviors associated with each specialty. First, we need to keep in mind that specialties are strengths; keeping this in mind avoids the pitfall of labeling a part of ourselves negatively.* What distinguishes the specialty column from the specialty in overuse column (page 82) is the overuse of the behaviors associated with the specialty (i.e., frequency of use, use in all contexts, and unconscious use), not the behaviors themselves. When we use behaviors repeatedly in a wide variety of situations and never look at their appropriateness, the behaviors become overused and some negative consequences may result.

To better understand each specialty and the specialty in overuse, we will describe the five specialties and the effects of their overuse, and list some flavors associated with each specialty in overuse.

---

*See Chapter 10 for a discussion of the dangers in doing this.

### Specialty 1: Analytic *(Adult Perspective)*

a. **Description:** A teacher with the *Analytic* specialty limits emotional responses to situations and people and focuses on facts. A teacher with the *Analytic* specialty is noted for being a very clear thinker even in difficult and emotionally charged situations. Teachers with the *Analytic* specialty are not reactive and not likely to elicit a reaction. They make good mediators and referees.

b. **Effects of Overuse:** A teacher who overuses this specialty may frustrate some students who want an emotional response from a teacher such as empathy or sympathy. A teacher who overuses this specialty can come across as stiff, unfeeling, robotic, or overly analytical. The teacher can also appear unreachable, incapable of feeling, distant, and aloof. If left unchecked, the teacher may have difficulty forming personal relationships with students or colleagues. Students may have difficulty relating to a teacher who is overusing this specialty. Teachers with this specialty may also bore others with unwanted or unrequested information.

c. **Flavors of Overuse:** emotionless, intellectual, unfeeling, insensitive, superior, robotic, controlled.

### Specialty 2: Helpful *(Supportive Parent Perspective)*

a. **Description:** A teacher with the *Helpful* specialty focuses on others and looks for what others need and want. A teacher with the *Helpful* specialty is very focused on student needs and is very supportive. A teacher with this specialty listens carefully to student problems and tries diligently to find solutions to the problems. This teacher is very often involved with students outside the classroom.

b. **Effects of Overuse:** A teacher who overuses this specialty often has trouble saying no and sometimes has too much activity in his or her life. *Helpful* teachers often find themselves involved in too many activities such as committees and out-of-class activities. They are often unable to allocate time to work-related projects that are near and dear to their hearts. A teacher with this specialty may also have difficulty asking for what he or she wants and therefore may come across as a martyr.

c. **Flavors of Overuse:** exhausted, frazzled, hassled, scattered, busy.

### *Specialty 3:* Influential *(Critical Parent Perspective)*

a. **Description:** A person with the *Influential* specialty focuses on excellence and on influencing others to be the best that they can be. A teacher with the *Influential* specialty has substantial information and knowledge about many things and is able to communicate this information easily to students and colleagues. Teachers with this specialty make excellent mentors and leaders. They are not only knowledgeable but are also connected to important contacts and people. They can also be delightfully irreverent.

b. **Effects of Overuse:** A teacher who overuses the *Influential* specialty can be wordy or long-winded in giving feedback because the teacher is so focused on excellence and giving students and colleagues the best and most detailed feedback and information possible. Students who communicate with a teacher with an *Influential* specialty may feel judged and criticized.

c. **Flavors of Overuse:** judgmental, critical, pushy, controlling, macho, bitchy, bullying, dominating, guru-like.

### *Specialty 4:* Playful *(Natural Child Perspective)*

a. **Description:** A person with the *Playful* specialty is fun to be around, is often described as uninhibited, and sees the world in unique ways. This person is usually quite relaxed and not stressed out. A teacher with the *Playful* specialty is also very willing to make mistakes, has an excellent sense of humor, and is often highly entertaining.

**b. Effects of Overuse:** A teacher who overuses this specialty may come across as somewhat flaky and without a serious side. This behavior makes it seem like the teacher is out of touch with reality because of laid back, humorous, and non-committal answers. Such behavior may frustrate students and colleagues because it appears that questions are not taken seriously. Students may feel that their concerns are not being addressed. A teacher who overuses the *Playful* specialty often focuses more on his or her responses than on the interaction that provoked the need to respond.

**c. Flavors of Overuse:** performer, joker, entertainer, goofy, dingy, easygoing, doesn't take anything seriously.

### Specialty 5: Sensitive *(Adapted Child Perspective)*

**a. Description:** A teacher with the *Sensitive* specialty has strong emotional responses to situations and easily recognizes his or her own feelings, as well as the feelings of students and colleagues. A teacher with the *Sensitive* specialty is concerned about students and responds empathetically to their questions and problems. Such a teacher comes across as being very safe.

**b. Effects of Overuse:** A teacher who overuses this specialty can come across as shy, fragile, and easily damaged. Sometimes the focus on fragility keeps *Sensitive* teachers from taking normal courses of action (i.e., a teacher is obviously upset but refuses to do anything about it). A teacher overusing this specialty may sit in meetings and listen to problems about which he or she has valuable input without saying anything. A teacher who overuses this specialty may also be very sensitive to how others feel or what they think and may, as a result, spend a lot of time justifying his or her actions or behavior, perhaps to deflect imagined criticism. Mood changes and inappropriate theatrical behavior are also associated with the overuse of the *Sensitive* specialty.

**c. Flavors of Overuse:** victim, tragedy queen, wimp, dramatic, shy, picked-on.

Our experience has been that it is generally easy to recognize specialties in others but not as easy to recognize specialties in oneself. To understand ourselves better as human beings and teachers, it is important to be able to identify specialties and to work with them in overuse, when applicable.

## IDENTIFYING SPECIALTIES IN OURSELVES

A first step in learning to work with specialties is being able to recognize them. Since specialties are ways of characterizing behaviors we use, it is logical to conclude that specialties should be obvious to the individual displaying them, but this is not always the case. In this light, one of our colleagues shared this story with us.

> One day, I went to a colleague for some advice and began to complain about another person in the department, listing all of the person's faults. My colleague stopped me and said, "This may sound harsh, but are you aware of how judgmental you sound? In fact, you may be creating the kind of antagonistic situation you are in right now. Your own judgments are causing many of your problems."

Our colleague told us that after that conversation, she started noticing her judgments. It became clear to her that her judgmental and superior behavior (associated with overuse of the *Influential* specialty) had been quite obvious to everyone around her, but she had been completely blind to it.

### Strategy 1: Observation

#### Noticing Your Reactions to Descriptions of Specialties

Thinking about your reactions to the descriptions of the specialties. Do some descriptions seem to fit? Can you think of instances when you use these behaviors? Do you feel more uncomfortable reading some of the descriptions than others? Those that make you feel the most uncomfortable are often those that fit the best. This simple introspective exercise may be enough for you to become conscious of your own specialties.

## Identifying Specialties in Other People

Observing specialties in other people is useful because it is often easier to recognize specialties exhibited by others rather than those we exhibit ourselves. This may be because we are less attached to and invested in other people's specialties (i.e., we have a neutral affective schemata and can easily engage our executive processes in the task).** We believe that identifying specialties in others is an important first step in identifying our own specialties.

### *Strategy 2: Using Feedback*

Another effective way to learn about specialties is through supportive feedback. The colleague whom we mentioned above hit the nail on the head relative to feedback: "Because of the nature of my friendship with the colleague who gave me feedback, because I asked for the feedback, because he provided it in a matter-of-fact way, and because he didn't set himself up as being in contrast to me, I was able to hear what he said without getting defensive."

In other words, if we trust the person who gives us feedback, if we ask for the feedback, if the feedback is provided in a supportive way, and when the person giving the feedback stays out of the way, feedback can be extremely useful. When feedback is given in this way, we do not feel inclined to deny or defend behaviors. In our lives as teachers, we have both sought feedback on our own specialties and have found the process useful. If it seems that obtaining feedback on your specialty might be useful to you and you can find a person to give it to you, here are some questions to answer to make the process work as smoothly as possible.

> **A. Why should I receive feedback?** Be clear about your purposes for receiving feedback. If you do not establish your purpose in advance, you may end up experiencing feedback as criticism. If you establish with the person providing feedback

---

**See Chapter 10 for a discussion of projection, the psychological principle underlying the relationship between our perceptions of others and of ourselves (von Franz, 1980).

that you want it to be offered in the context of encouragement and support so that you can achieve your full potential, you will likely be able to let the feedback sink in.

**B. Where should I receive feedback?** Decide for yourself where you will feel most comfortable receiving feedback. For some people an office seems too sterile, and many teachers prefer feedback sessions to be informal, taking place in a café or restaurant. In addition, most of us prefer feedback sessions to be private with just one other person, since for many, receiving feedback in a group may feel more threatening.

**C. When should I receive feedback?** For most people, feedback is easiest to hear when we specifically ask for it as opposed to when it is volunteered without our asking or forced on us as part of an evaluation process. Notice when you are feeling open to feedback and ask for it at that time. You might also consider the time of day (e.g., if you're a morning person, meeting with someone before work may be better than having a session at the end of the day).

**D. How should I receive feedback?** Ask the person giving you feedback to phrase it in a certain way so it is easier for you to hear. For example, you may find it easier to hear feedback when it is expressed positively ("I'd like to see you do more. . . .") rather than negatively ("You are too ___ or not enough ___."). You might also ask the person giving you feedback to balance it (i.e., talk about your strengths as well as the behaviors that may be getting in your way). There are perhaps phrases or strategies that might work for you. Think about what would work best for you and instruct the person giving you feedback in how to do it.

**E. How much feedback should I receive?** You must decide on the amount and type of feedback you wish to receive. Since many teachers have told us that they are sensitive about their specialties, it might be wise to only receive a small amount of feedback at a time. You can always get more feedback later when you are ready to deal with it.

**F. From whom should I receive feedback?** Finally, and perhaps most important, is the issue of from whom to receive feedback. It is important to receive feedback from people you trust and with whom you feel comfortable. If you know people who are very diplomatic, whom you admire, or whom you use as role models, these would be good people to ask for feedback.

### Strategy 3:  Creating a Specialties Profile

A specialty profile is a graphic representation of the range of use of each specialty when used effectively and in overuse. Figure 6.1 shows one format for such a representation.

In this profile, the individual has two particularly noticeable specialties he uses in teaching—*Analytic* and *Playful;* these are both marked for extensive use on the bar graph. In terms of this teacher's self-analysis for overuse, we see that he has noted moderate overuse of *Analytic.* A careful, ongoing audit of behavior in this area would be beneficial for a teacher with this profile. In terms of the overuse of *Playful,* we note only an occasional overuse, so in terms of the self-analysis, this teacher does not view the specialty *Playful* as a problem. The specialties *Helpful* and *Sensitive* are used only occasionally. This teacher has determined that there is no overuse of the specialty *Helpful* and only an occasional overuse of *Sensitive.* It is interesting to note that this teacher does not see himself having any of the characteristics of the *Influential* specialty except in its occasional overuse toward the flavor Judgmental.

We believe that all teachers can benefit from an audit of teaching specialties, regardless of whether the overall profile is fairly balanced or one that the individual/teacher thinks needs some adjustment. The process makes us more aware of the behaviors we exhibit in the classroom and in our interactions with students and colleagues. Specialties contribute to our successes as teachers, but in overuse they may contribute to our inability to achieve our potential as teachers.

**Figure 6.1**    Example Specialties Profile

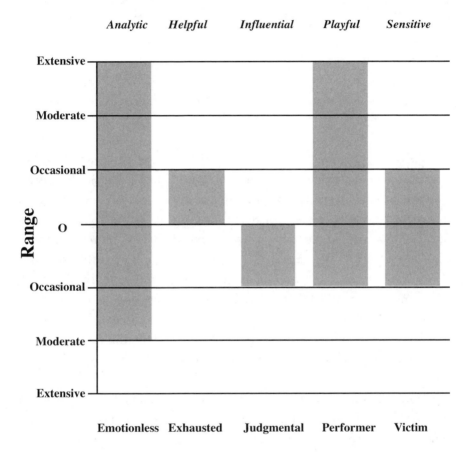

## WORKING WITH SPECIALTIES IN OVERUSE

Based on the audit of your teaching specialties, you may decide that you want to make adjustments in your profile. We use two general approaches for working with specialties in overuse: centering and rounding out.[5]

### Centering

A centering strategy involves reducing the use of existing behaviors. The advantage of the centering strategy is that it does not require the development of new abilities.

We used this strategy with a teacher who overused the *Playful* specialty (e.g., he spent too much time joking or story-telling in class). He was an effective teacher in many ways but almost always got off track with his jokes and stories, many of which were lost on his language students. In fact, in his course evaluations, students noted that he didn't take their concerns seriously. We suggested the centering strategy with this teacher and asked him to try to avoid the temptation to joke and tell stories for a while. Instead, we asked that he make a note of each time he was tempted to do so and what the positive and negative consequences of doing so might be in that situation. After the teacher had done this for a while, he became more aware of important considerations affecting his decisions to joke.[6]

While we have found this strategy to be very valuable, we to want to note one caveat. Some people consider the suggestion "not to do something" a judgment of their personality or of who they are. For this reason, prior to making any such suggestions, we make certain to help the teacher focus on our positive intention behind the suggestion.

### Rounding Out

The second strategy we have used successfully in making adjustments in the overuse of specialties in teaching is called rounding out. This strategy involves developing or adding new abilities or behaviors to supplement the behaviors associated with one's specialty.

One strength of this strategy is that it focuses on the positive. Instead of saying, "Don't do this" (overused specialty), we say, "Do this" (new ability). For example, if a teacher is already highly organized and clear about what she or he is teaching but tends to come across as unfeeling, we might suggest that the teacher spend a few minutes of each class asking students more personal questions about the concepts being taught, including giving their ideas and opinion. Asking personal questions might be a new behavior for a teacher who typically behaved in a fairly impersonal manner.

We have used this strategy with another teacher with the *Playful* specialty. This teacher used her *Playful* specialty, which manifested as a sense of humor, instead of preparing adequately, and when we watched her teach, it was clear to us that she was not preparing adequately. She did many good things as a teacher. She interacted well with her students and managed the class well; we could see that she genuinely cared about her students. However, she didn't know the course content well, and she always seemed to be looking for things because her materials were unorganized. When we talked to her about her teaching, she told us that when she was very well organized and prepared, she didn't feel spontaneous or creative; however, her spontaneous actions often backfired. We suggested first of all that being prepared did not mean that she had to give up her spontaneity, humor, and creativity. We then asked her to identify the things she liked about herself as a teacher. We suggested that she keep all of those qualities in her teaching and add being well prepared to her palette. She identified new behaviors and saw them as adding to rather than subtracting from.

We can use the organizing principles already involved in classifying specialties to characterize useful kinds of behaviors to add in order to round out existing behaviors. Figure 6.2 suggests one possible set of relationships between existing specialties and other specialties that tend to round them out.

For example, a teacher with a *Playful* specialty might add some behaviors more characteristic of the *Analytic* specialty. A teacher with an *Influential* specialty might add behaviors more characteristic of the *Playful* specialty. However, although we suggest changing behaviors associated with specialties in order to balance one's overall profile and become more effective educators, we do not wish to give the impression that such changes

**Figure 6.2**   Some Alternative Perspectives

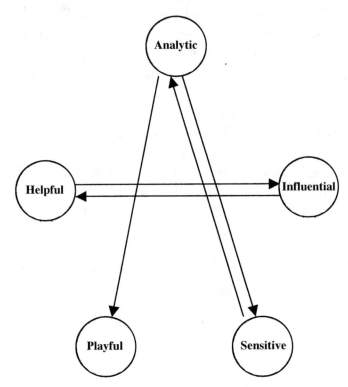

are necessarily easy to make. After all, we have probably had most of a lifetime's experience in using the behaviors associated with these specialties and, perhaps, avoiding the underlying issues that drive them. Even though a discussion of probable causes for these behaviors is beyond the scope and focus of this book, we do recognize that there are underlying causes and fears that drive behaviors, many of which we may not be aware. As we have noted, in this book we do not provide ways to delve into the past to uncover and work therapeutically with experiences that may have contributed to the formation of specialties.

Before and after versions of the specialty profile illustrated in Figure 6.1 can be used to assess specialty-related aspects of teacher development. Figure 6.3 shows one teacher's self-assessment of her specialty profile before she started to focus on her specialties and after she had worked on alternatives for a period of time.

**Figure 6.3**    An Example of Teacher Development

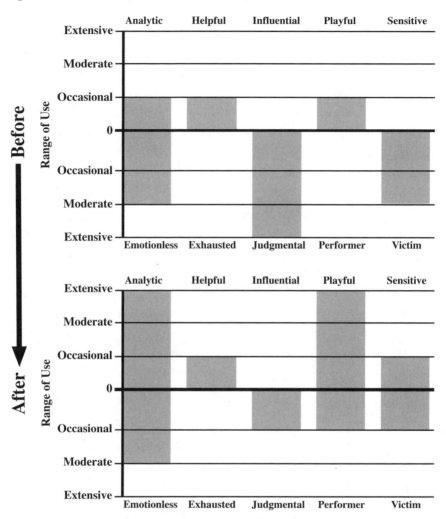

This chapter presented a view of teaching specialties and how they interface with internal perspectives. In this view, there is no value attached to any internal perspective or teaching specialty. However, we also recognize that the ability to determine how to respond to one's environment depends on one not being controlled by an overuse of a specialty. Because teaching puts us into contact with people under conditions that can be stressful, it has the potential to create the very conditions in which we overuse our specialties. As teachers we want to decide when and how to use our specialties without being controlled by them. Teaching creates a mirror (an often-used metaphor) we can use to become more conscious of and work with our specialties.

Learning to use our specialties to our advantage in both our professional and personal lives, however, does not happen overnight. We might learn the same lessons or different versions of them over and over. As we continue to learn, the lessons stop being such a big deal and start feeling like gentle reminders rather than rude awakenings. Who we are unfolds in each moment of our lives in fresh, creative, and unique ways. If we are open to it, this unfolding will not be conditioned or limited by specialties in overuse. It will be enhanced by our appropriate use of them.[7]

Finally, we need to emphasize there are no good or bad specialties. Nor is there a good or bad or right or wrong way to live with one's specialties. Many great contributions have been made by people with a very narrow focus and range of behaviors. However, the more you are controlled by one specialty in overuse, the more you limit the range of interactions you can have with others (Richo, 1991). It is up to each individual teacher to determine what to do with this information.

## NOTES

1. These characteristics of specialties correspond in many ways to the construct "neurotic style" in the field of psychology (Shapiro, 1989, 2000). For an overview of research into the trait structure of personality (a way of thinking about specialties), including research on the validity of putative traits, see Carver and Scheier (2000) and Friedman and Schustack (2002). We were introduced to many of the references on neurotic style by Madeline Ehrman (2000).

2. There exists a wide variety of systems and instruments for classifying and identifying personality traits that might correspond to specialties. One well-known system is the MMPI (Hathaway & McKinley, 2003). For two other systems, see Millon (2006) and Shapiro (1965, 1989). For an overview of perspectives on personality, see Carver and Scheier (2000) and Friedman and Schustack (2002). For applying the MMPI in the classroom, see Fairhurst and Fairhurst (1995).

3. While this book is not about the origins of behaviors, transactional analysts hypothesize that the origin of what we call overuse of specialties stem from the

Adapted Child ego state that has modified its behavior under Parental influence. The Adapted Child "...behaves as father (or mother) wanted him to behave: compliantly or precociously, for example. Or he adapts himself by withdrawing or whining. Thus, the Parental influence is a cause and the Adapted Child an effect" (Berne, 1964, p. 26). In this book, rather than locating the adapted behaviors that constitute the specialties in overuse in the Adapted Child ego state, we have found it pedagogically useful to locate them in various perspectives, which calls attention to their forms rather than their origins. The result of this is that the behaviors we associate with the Adapted Child perspective in our framework are less varied than those associated with the Adapted Child in transactional analysis.

4. The more general observation that the behavior in the specialty elicits the kind of feelings that the person with the specialty tries to avoid has not gone unnoticed and is, in fact, encapsulated in the well-known maxim, "what you resist persists." For example, Teacher A admitted that she acted helpful because she was afraid that she wasn't inherently valued and needed to do something to create the experience of being valued, and she chose being helpful as a way of doing so. However, the more she acted helpful to avoid the feeling of not being valued, the less inherently valued she felt because she didn't give herself the opportunity to be valued for herself and not for all of her helpful behavior.

5. A third general way to work with specialties is to examine the past to uncover experiences that may have contributed to the origin of the specialty and then attempt to resolve these issues. This process may involve discovering a self-doubt or fear that one continues to try to avoid by acting out through the overuse of the specialty, and then finding a way to work directly with the underlying issue. For example, a self-doubt or fear that might underlie the *Performing* specialty might be, "I'm afraid I don't matter just as I am" (so I need to perform to be noticed and valued). Therapeutic approaches for investigating past causes of present behaviors such as this are, as we indicated, beyond the scope of this book.

6. With respect to the centering strategy, which involves not doing rather than doing, the following observations seem relevant to us. In Chapter 1, we discussed Campbell's view of an authentic life as following one's bliss by doing things in one's life that are nearest and dearest to one's heart. The idea of authenticity in one's life can be approached from a variety of directions (for a number of different characterization of authenticity, see Nagel, 2000). From a psychological point of view, we might consider an authentic life to be one in which one's behavior is not associated with compulsive or unconscious overuse of a specialty. In other words, an authentic life is not one associated with any particular kind of behavior but with the *absence* of compulsive or highly predictable behavior. We were first introduced to the idea of defining authenticity in terms of an absence in Broadbent

(1976) who studied characteristics of individuals who were generally well liked by others. Broadbent found that it was not what these individuals did that they had in common but instead what they did not do: They did not try to be liked (p. 17). If one associates the unconscious or compulsive use of a specialty with an indirect request for acceptance or recognition (which one does not try to do if one is living an authentic life in Campbell's sense), the specialty in overuse can be seen as a link between Broadbent's hypothesis and Campbell's idea of an authentic life. Of course, it is not necessary to always be authentic or to make this some sort of rule. However, we think it is useful to have the authentic option available.

7. You may find out as you work with your specialty that what you learn may end up being one of your greatest strengths. For example, we have a colleague whose specialty played out in his being continually angry and critical. After becoming aware of this and making a concentrated effort to develop alternative strategies, he has become one of the university's safest and most expert negotiators. However, he has kept the strength in his criticalness in his ability to positively influence the course of events.

"Although the actions of living organisms can be described from the viewpoint of an objective observer, such a description misses the most striking characteristic of animate behavior: its orientation toward some goal or purpose."

Gary Cziko
*Without Miracles: Universal Selection Theory and
the Second Darwinian Revolution*
(2000, p. 242)

# Chapter 7

# Values Clarification and Goal-Setting

Chapters 2–6 investigated some characteristics of the internal world (e.g., affective schemata, internal perspectives, and teaching specialties) that influence how we typically respond to the external world and determine whether or not we are able to experience our teaching lives as satisfaction, pleasure, or privilege. Chapter 7 focuses on two additional characteristics of the internal world, values and goals, and on the specific processes associated with them, namely, values clarification and goal-setting.

To clarify values and set goals, we must interact with time, one of the most important characteristics of the external world. The importance of values clarification and goal-setting in relationship to time is aptly depicted in this story entitled, "The Mason Jar."

One day an expert in time management was speaking to a group of business students and, to drive home a point, used an illustration those students will never forget. As he stood in front of the group of high-powered overachievers he said, "Okay, time for a quiz."

He pulled out a one-gallon, wide-mouthed mason jar and set it on the table in front of him. Then he produced about a dozen fist-sized rocks and carefully placed them, one at a time, into the jar. When the jar was filled to the top and no more rocks would fit inside, he asked, "Is this jar full?" Everyone in the class said, "Yes." Then he said, "Really?"

He reached under the table and pulled out a bucket of gravel. Then he dumped some gravel in and shook the jar causing pieces of gravel to work themselves down into the space between the big rocks. Then he asked the group once more, "Is the jar full?" By this time the class was on to him.

"Probably not," one of them answered. "Good!" he replied. He reached under the table and brought out a bucket of sand. He started dumping the sand in the jar, and it went into all of the spaces left between the rocks and the gravel. Once more he asked the question, "Is this jar full?"

"No!" the class shouted. Once again he said, "Good." Then he grabbed a pitcher of water and began to pour it in until the jar was filled to the brim. Then he looked at the class and asked, "What is the point of this illustration?"

One eager beaver raised his hand and said, "The point is, no matter how full your schedule is, if you try really hard you can always fit some more things in it!"

"No," the speaker replied. "That's <u>not</u> the point. The truth this illustration teaches us is that if you don't put the big rocks in first, you'll never get them in at all." What are the big rocks in your life—Your children? Your loved ones? Your education? Your dreams? A worthy cause? Teaching or mentoring others? Doing things that you love? Time for yourself? Your health? Your significant other?

Remember to put the big rocks in first or you'll never get them in at all. If you sweat the little stuff (the gravel, the sand), then you'll fill your life with little things you worry about that don't really matter, and you'll never have the real quality time you need to spend on the big, important stuff (the big rocks).

(Author unknown[1])

It is through the processes of values clarification and goal-setting that we identify what is most important in our lives, and what is most important goes into the mason jar before anything else. Without making time to focus on our values and goals, we may not be able to create a life that is full of what is most important to us and around which all other life activity revolves.

There are two main reasons why we may resist the processes of values clarification and goal-setting. First, we get caught up in the processes of organizing and tracking activity in our daily lives and on the technology related to these events (i.e., the materials we select for keeping track of daily events). The belief that some individuals hold is that personal organizers or computers are essential to the process of managing one's time and that it is impossible to be effective without this technological support. However, this has not been our experience. We have found the most important part of organizing and managing one's time is the values and goal-setting processes, not the technology for keeping track of daily events. Paper-and-pencil day planners, simple calendars, lists, or electronic management systems can all work equally well.

Another reason that teachers may resist these processes is because they often feel more productive when tracking and organizing daily events. It is natural to feel that we don't have time in our busy lives to clarify our values and set goals. Both of us resisted these processes ourselves in the beginning, feeling that it was more important to get on with the daily business of tracking and organizing activity in our lives. For example, "When I first became a language program administrator, I felt like I had lost control of my life. Every second of every work day was so full of tasks on my to do list that I scarcely had time to think. I continually complained about not having time to write and do the things that really mattered to me. When someone suggested that I take a course on managing my time and take time to think about my own goals and values, I felt criticized and wanted to scream in frustration. I could hardly find time to eat, so how could I find time to take a course and quiet time to think about my goals and values?" It is hard at first to make the connection between the processes of values clarification and goal-setting and managing one's time. In fact, one almost has to participate in these processes first before the connection becomes clear. However, our experience has been that if you don't begin with values clarification and goal-setting, the chances are very good you will spend your time on activity that may not be important to what you value and want in your life. In the end you will feel frustrated and burned out.

Chapter 7 can be used as a type of instruction manual. We hope you will read through the materials initially to get a complete picture of the processes of values clarification and goal-setting. Then after the first reading, we hope you will be able to use the materials as a reference and resource, selecting material that is most relevant and useful to you in your own process of values clarification and goal-setting.

## GOVERNING VALUES

Governing values describe actual or anticipated virtues, traits, or behaviors that you consider most important in your life. Researchers and writers have defined governing values in different ways. For example, Winwood describes a governing value operationally as an affirmation that answers the question, "If I were living that value perfectly, what would my behavior be like?" (Winwood, 1990, p. 48). Governing values also encapsulate our highest priorities (i.e., what we stand for, what we think, believe, and know) and our strongest beliefs (paraphrase from Winwood, 1990, p. 41–42).[2] Ralph Waldo Emerson also made the same point when he said that, "Nothing gives so much direction to a person's life as a set of sound principles." In summary, governing values provide a means for regulating our lives and developing satisfying goals that we can relate directly to those values. When we go through our professional and personal lives in a deliberate way, we can then reference our behaviors to our goals and our underlying governing values.

Governing values differ from individual to individual, and what is valuable to one person may or may not be valuable to another. For this reason, each teacher must look within herself or himself to discover governing values and not look for some external standard. For example, in the area of finances, one individual may value risk-taking, an extravagant lifestyle, and making a lot of money, whereas, another individual may value conservative financial management and saving money. Each of us must discover for ourselves what we value and then learn how to structure our daily activities to derive maximum satisfaction from them.[3]

In addition to variation among individuals, governing values can change within the individual over time; what is important to us this year may not be important to us in a decade. For example, one of our colleagues, a full professor in a top-ranked American university, spent much of his early and middle career years at the cutting edge of his field, writing and developing new paradigms for considering his subject matter. Later on, his emphasis shifted to working with graduate students, helping them to pursue their interests. He no longer felt the same need to do research. Realizing that governing values are dynamic should help us accept where we are without feeling like we have some sort of lifelong obligation to stand by our current values.

Before beginning the process of discovering your own governing values, it is useful to think in general about the possible areas of focus for these values. This list contains some common areas of focus for governing values.

| | |
|---|---|
| • Adventure | • Love of God |
| • Appreciation of diversity | • Love of music |
| • Contribution | • Love of nature |
| • Courage | • Love/closeness |
| • Creativity | • Non-judgment |
| • Deliberateness | • Organization |
| • Directness (non-manipulation) | • Personal growth |
| • Emotional safety | • Piety |
| • Enthusiasm | • Playfulness |
| • Evenness | • Risk-taking |
| • Frugality | • Self-acceptance |
| • Generosity | • Self-control |
| • Health | • Sense of humor |
| • Humor | • Serving others |
| • Impeccability | • Spirituality |
| • Inclusion | • Spontaneity |
| • Individuality | • Stylishness |
| • Kindness | • Taking responsibility |
| • Learning/growth | • Trusting myself |

## Discovering Your Own Governing Values

We believe that the chances of making rewarding decisions and experiencing your career as pleasure, satisfaction, and privilege are greatly enhanced by articulating your governing values, and many teachers have told us that they have benefited from the process of making governing values explicit. This is particularly true for new and inexperienced teachers or teachers who may not be experiencing their careers as fulfilling. A process we have found most useful for discovering governing values is one many writers and educators use and it includes questioning, brainstorming, revising, consolidating, and finding evidence. The process works best if used repeatedly over time; however, the results of the process may vary over time because governing values are always a work in progress. Keeping the ever-changing nature of governing values in mind removes some of the stress that might be associated with thinking that a list of values is definitive, or right or wrong. Some steps in the discovery process that we hope will be useful to you follow.

1. **Ask yourself a question.**
   a. On a blank sheet of paper, write the following question: If I am living the kind of life I really want to live, what actual or anticipated virtues, traits, or strengths would be most important for me?
   b. Tape this paper to the wall in front of you.
2. **Brainstorm.**
   a. Set a timer for five minutes.
   b. Write down every thought that comes to mind in response to this question.
   c. Keep your pencil (or typing fingers) moving at all times.
   d. Do not censor your thoughts in any way.
   e. Do not reject thoughts that seem to be off topic.
3. **Take a break.**
   a. Leave the list alone for 5 to 30 minutes.
4. **Revise.**
   a. Read over what you wrote.
   b. Cross out material that is not on topic.
   c. Keep a copy of the original.

### 5. Consolidate.

a. Prepare a sign with the following message: "I do not have to take everything into account right now." You can keep this list and decide to focus on part of it. In addition, you can always incorporate more items at a later time. Deleting items does not mean that they are gone forever.

b. Ask yourself this question: "If I had to focus on 6 to 15 of these values right now, which ones would I focus on?"

c. Take 15 minutes to reduce your list to 6 to 15 values.

d. Start each item in the list with the following:

"An important part of me highly values _____."

### 6. Find evidence of your governing value.

a. Write a one-sentence description of how you know when you are acting in harmony with each value (see examples).

b. Revise and update your governing values every month or so until they become stable. Keep in mind that governing values are not rules to follow but points of reference to consider when making decisions about what to do.

## Evidence of Governing Values

Some examples of governing values and descriptions of behaviors that let you know when you are acting in accordance with the values that you have identified in the discovery process follow. Note that these governing values are more about reference points for behavior than about specific goals you may want to achieve.

**Adventure:** I leap at opportunities to undertake new projects.

**Humor:** I enjoy laughing at life and at myself.

**Individuality:** I see my own points of view and those of others as unique.

**Learning/growth/creativity:** I look for and am open to learning from my experiences.

**Love of music:** I search for and notice opportunities to incorporate music into my work and play.

### Working with Important Concepts and Terms

To refine the list of governing values you created in the discovery process and talk about governing values and their relationship to the overall process of organizing and managing one's time, we introduce several technical terms who will be helpful: *domain, role models, goals, tasks,* and *routines. Domains* consist of different contexts for behavior. In other words, they provide an organizational structure for your governing values. *Role models* are individuals who serve as examples of people who manifest the ideal behaviors you have described. *Goals* are specific, measurable outcomes that you want to achieve by a specified point in time. *Tasks* are "activit(ies) that involve individuals in using time for the purpose of achieving a particular goal, in a particular situation" (Bachman & Palmer, 1996, p. 44). *Routines* are repeated sets of tasks that will allow you to function efficiently within each domain.

The chart shows how these different concepts and terms fit together.

| Core Domains | Goals | Tasks |
|---|---|---|
| **Domain 1** *Profession* | Professional goals | Professional tasks |
| **Domain 2** *Relationships* | Relationship goals | Relationship tasks |
| **Domain 3** *Health & Fitness* | Health and fitness goals | Health & fitness tasks |
| **Domain 4** *Finances* | Finances goals | Finances tasks |
| **Domain 5** *Recreation* | Recreation goals | Recreation tasks |
| **Domain 6** *Personal Education* | Personal education goals | Personal education tasks |
| **Domain 7** *Basic Support Systems* | Basic support systems goals | Basic support systems tasks |

## Core Domains

While there are many ways to divide one's life into domains, we have found the seven core domains that follow to be widely applicable and general enough to account for the different ways in which many teachers organize and use their time. Descriptions of these core domains that we have found useful in working with teachers follow.

- **Profession.** The profession domain includes activities associated primarily with your work. Since the primary focus of this book is on the teaching profession, we will devote extra time to it.

- **Relationships.** The relationships domain includes activities associated primarily with creating and maintaining friendships, married life or partnerships, and immediate and extended family.

- **Health and fitness.** The health and fitness domain includes activities associated primarily with creating the kind of physical abilities that you want to maintain, such as playing tennis or golf, running, hiking, etc.

- **Finances.** The financial domain includes activities associated with creating financial resources and systems for managing these resources.

- **Recreation.** The recreation domain includes activities associated with play, hobbies, and renewal/relaxation such as going to movies, watching TV, and taking trips.

- **Personal education.** The personal education domain includes activities associated with creating and maintaining the internal resources you need to understand yourself and conduct your life consistent with this self-awareness. Personal education is education about the self, such as reading a book that interests you or traveling to a foreign country to take a language course.

- **Basic support systems.** The basic support systems domain includes activities associated primarily with creating and maintaining an environment conducive to pursuing and completing goals in other areas; thus, the value of this domain is distributed over other domains. Some specific basic support systems within this domain include creating and maintaining your shelter, clothing, transportation, and communication, as well as managing time. While creating these systems can be satisfying in their own right, their primary function is enabling us to function efficiently in the other domains. Note that the financial domain logically fits in the support system domain, but financial management is typically complex enough to warrant considering it a separate domain for the purposes of organizing and managing one's time.

You may want to add other core domains or conceive of domains in a slightly different way, and there is no problem with either approach. We suggest starting with the core domains and making adjustments and modifications as your personal process and system unfolds. Think of domains and the concept of managing time within the framework of your entire life and try to keep the list of core domains to a manageable number.

You will also note that the example core domains presented include domains that extend beyond those that teachers generally associate with their professional lives. As stated in Chapters 1 and 2, our professional and personal lives are intimately connected and what we learn in one area informs the other. Stress often results when we are unable to balance our professional and personal lives. Thus, to make effective decisions about how to manage our professional lives, we need to consider how the decisions we make fit within the context of our lives as a whole.

### Principles for Managing Time in the Various Domains*

To effectively integrate the domains into a system for organizing and managing time, we offer three principles to guide you in this process.

---

*The principles provided are derived from Bachman & Palmer's thinking about principles for using qualities of useful language tests (Bachman & Palmer, 1996, Chapter 2.).

### Principle 1: Interactivity

Because the domains interact, whatever is experienced in one domain will affect goals accomplished and levels of satisfaction in other domains. You may notice this interaction when you have some difficulty determining whether a particular goal belongs in one domain or another. For example, suppose you decide to collaborate with a number of personal friends in putting on a professional workshop. You may find yourself wondering whether the goal belongs in the Profession or the Relationships domain, since the goal seems to contribute to both (i.e., you know that you will benefit professionally and also expand your friendships in the process of putting on the workshop). By recognizing that the domains interact, you can feel free to put the goal in either domain. In a similar manner, improving communication skills can improve relationships or teaching, and getting feedback on your teaching can improve your ability to communicate in your relationships.

### Principle 2: Overall Management of Resources in the Domains

It is the *overall* management of time in all of the domains that should be improved, rather than the management of time in one or a selected number of individual domains. Therefore, when managing your time, it is more effective to focus on all of the domains collectively. For example, if you decide that your entire life is about your work and you pour all of your energy into work, you are likely to find that your relationships, home environment, financial management, physical fitness, and health will suffer.

### Principle 3: No "Correct" Way to Allocate Resources

There is no correct way to allocate resources in the different domains. The overall management of time and the appropriate balance of the use of time in the different domains cannot be prescribed in general but must be determined by each individual. Therefore, do not assume that how someone else manages his or her time will be the most effective way to manage your own. The management of time in the various domains cannot be prescribed in general but must be developed by a specific person at a particular time in that person's life. The amount of energy we give to various domains in our lives changes over time depending on what is going on in our lives.

### Ideal Behaviors

Once you have established your core domains, the next stop is to operationalize them in terms of ideal behaviors. Ideal behaviors are short descriptions of how you behave or what you aspire to do when you are performing at your best in a particular domain. These ideal behaviors embody your governing values within a particular domain and can be used as reference points against which to evaluate your actual behaviors.

Create preliminary descriptions of your ideal behaviors in each of the domains you have chosen. You may find it helpful to use essentially the same process that we outlined for discovering your governing values. Make a rough draft, set it aside, then look at it and revise as necessary for a couple of weeks. Compare your list of actual behaviors with this list of ideal behaviors in order to help you understand how consistent your actual behavior is with your governing values.

### Example Ideal Behaviors

Example descriptions of ideal behaviors and actual behaviors in several of the core domains follow. When the behaviors are presented side-by-side, it is easy to see how actual behaviors may be inconsistent with one's ideal behaviors and, ultimately, with one's governing values.

The example domains show the comparison of ideal behaviors with actual behaviors. In the profession domain, some of the actual behaviors are consistent with the ideal behaviors. In the relationships domain, almost all of the actual behaviors are consistent with the ideal behaviors. However, in the health and fitness domain, none of the actual behaviors are consistent with the ideal behaviors. Comparing actual behaviors with ideal behaviors in each of the domains you have identified is an efficient way of identifying the behaviors you want to work on and ultimately change.

| Ideal Behaviors for Profession Domain | Actual Behaviors for Profession Domain |
|---|---|
| I engage in intellectually challenging learning and in creative problem solving. I enjoy making sense of new situations. I tell the truth and treat students equitably. I accept where students are and help them build on that according to their goals and abilities. I am open to criticism from others and acknowledge their points of view. | I find very little of my own work intellectually challenging. I enjoy making sense of new situations, but I have little opportunity to do so. I have difficulty accepting my students just as they are. To avoid confrontation, I sometimes avoid telling students the truth. I treat all students equitably. |
| **Ideal Behaviors for Relationships Domain** | **Actual Behaviors for Relationships Domain** |
| I maintain supportive, fulfilling relationships. I accept others as they are and appreciate every person's unique contributions. I value humor. I work to create closeness, support, and mutual appreciation in my relationships. I spend quality time with and pay attention to my friends. I communicate openly and try to find solutions to problems. I minimize participating in gossip. I make a point to talk to people with few friends. | I maintain supportive, fulfilling relationships. I accept others as they are and appreciate every person's unique contributions. I value humor. I work to create closeness, support, and mutual appreciation in my relationships. I spend very little quality time with my friends. I communicate openly and come from solution. I often gossip. I make a point to talk to people with few friends. |
| **Ideal Behaviors for Health and Fitness Domain** | **Actual Behaviors for Health and Fitness Domain** |
| I do regular strength, aerobic, and stretching exercises. I eat a high-protein, low-glycemic, carbohydrate diet that gives me good energy. I maintain my ideal body weight and ideal body fat percentage. I get enough sleep, take regular relaxation breaks during the day, and get regular physical examinations. | I seldom do strength, aerobic, and stretching exercises. I eat too many sweets and glycemic carbohydrates at work. I am 15 pounds overweight. I don't get sufficient sleep on weeknights. I haven't had a physical exam for three years. |

### Role Models

Many people find the process of identifying role models to be useful in clarifying governing values. Role models are individuals who exemplify the ideal behaviors associated with your governing values in a particular domain. Role models can be people whom you know or individuals you have heard or read about. By identifying role models, you can create reference points for reflecting on ideal behaviors. Role models can show you that what you aspire to is possible. Mendelsohn describes the potential effects of role models:

> We have all, at some point in our lives, met or read about an individual whose ideas, behavior, or values have had a profound effect on us—a person we would call 'inspirational' or a 'role model.' These people have moved us, perhaps inspired us to try new things, or empowered us to take bolder steps than we would normally take. (Mendelsohn, 1998, p. 2)

One always has to be careful not to idealize role models or any individual for that matter.[5] Because role models are real people, they are fallible and make mistakes just as everyone does. In addition, a role model may also be inconsistent in the exemplification of governing values. Individuals who might be excellent role models for some governing values might be poor examples for others. To some extent, success in one area may have come at the expense of another.[6] Keep in mind that identifying role models is not critical to the process of values clarification. Rather, it is intended to be an option that can help you in the process of describing ideal behaviors.

## GOALS

Goals are specific, measurable outcomes that you want to achieve by a specified point in time. They are usually broad in scope, like projects, and completing them requires an extended application of effort over a period time. Goals provide the link or bridge between governing values and tasks because they help us experience the activity involved in the tasks as valuable. Moreover, setting goals that fully challenge our abilities allows us to experience flow when executing tasks associated with these goals (see the discussion of flow in Chapter 3). We present this bridge as a visual metaphor in Figure 7.1.

### Strategies for Achieving Goals

Robert Sternberg's definition of intelligence (1985) helped us understand more about the goal-setting process. Sternberg defined intelligence as "The purposeful adaptation to, selection of, and shaping of real-world environments relevant to one's life and abilities" (Sternberg 1988, p. 44). According to Sternberg's theory, we can interact with the external world in three ways: by selecting from the environment, shaping the environment to fit our needs and purposes, or adapting ourselves to fit the environment. Thus, selecting, adapting to, and modifying one's environment are the three strategies one can use for achieving goals.

#### Selecting

*Selecting* from your external environment means deciding whether or not to interact at all with a given environment. For example, let's suppose you love to write and publish what you have written, and that you need to do so to feel fulfilled. At the very basic level, it would make more sense to put some energy into selecting a job in which writing and publishing are valued rather than to select a job in which no importance is attached to writing and publishing.

**Figure 7.1**   The Purpose of Goals

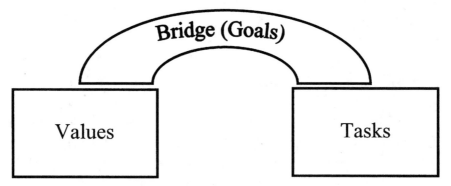

## Shaping

*Shaping* an environment involves interacting with it in such a way that the environment itself changes along the lines you want. It would be reasonable to use this strategy if in reflecting on the characteristics of the environment you decided that these characteristics were amenable to shaping, given the resources you were willing to put into the process. For example, let's say that you love music and have a talent for singing and playing the guitar. Let's also say that you love to teach. You might want to shape your professional environment so that you are able to include both of these activities in your life.

## Adapting

*Adapting* to the environment involves making changes within yourself to become in greater harmony with characteristics of the environment. For example, let's say that one of your goals is to teach in a particular school district because you admire the administration and so many of the teachers. If you work in this district and public school, district policies, however, will require you to carry out several tasks you detest. The big picture suggests that you might want to do the tasks rather than put a lot of energy into changing the policies all at once—particularly if the policies would be difficult to change in the short term. Adapting to the environment might be the most intelligent course of action; you could routinely complete the tasks while developing a plan and a timeline for changing the policies.

### *Deciding Which Strategy to Apply*

We are not aware of any all-purpose formula for deciding when to apply each of these three strategies (i.e., selecting, shaping, and adapting). In thinking about our own experiences as teachers, we realized that adapting was perhaps the most difficult of the three strategies to employ; yet, it is possibly the most powerful and rewarding. We believe this is the case because success in adapting to the environment requires that we change ourselves, and our ability to change depends to a large extent on understanding ourselves.

For example, a common fear that we had as new teachers was centered on developing an ability to answer student questions (i.e., What if I get questions that I cannot answer?). We experimented with a number of different strategies. One such strategy involved trying to shape the individuals and systems in the classrooms by creating rules, such as asking students to write their technical questions on a piece of paper and submit them in a question box for the next class period. We justified this strategy by claiming that we had so much material to cover and wanted to handle questions efficiently. Spontaneous questions took the class time away from concepts central to the course. In actuality, we wanted questions in advance in order to prepare answers. For new teachers trying to survive, the response and the attempt to shape the environment make sense. Of course, as you might guess, student responses to this shaping were not always positive. We have also used more subtle approaches to dealing with our fears about student questions. We simply allowed no time for questions, or we changed the content to focus on familiar and easy material that would not cause students to ask challenging questions. Doing the former is frustrating to students, and doing the latter waters down the curriculum.

While shaping may be our first response to difficult situations, adapting may be a better long-term solution. We might adapt to our students by encouraging their questions and, more important, by admitting that we don't know all the answers (if we don't), and continuing to learn about ourselves and our profession in the process. Decisions to adapt to students by changing internally often come later in the development of teachers and coincide with our development as individuals.

Professional goals that are achieved through selecting from one's environment might involve finding a different job or moving to a different department within one's job. Professional goals that are achieved through modifying one's environment might involve creating and teaching a new course, writing a book in an attempt to influence how people work within their environments, or giving a professional presentation to influence how people teach. Professional goals that are achieved through adapting to one's professional environment might involve learning how to get along with a difficult department member or learning how to do a new and required task. To achieve goals, we must be able to access and use the strategies of selecting, modifying, or adapting in relation to the goals we set in order to have a choice in how we approach achieving goals. In other words, we must decide if the specific goal we set is best achieved by adapting to our environment, selecting from it, or modifying it.

The focus must always be on using the strategies to achieve goals and not on using the strategies to avoid facing a difficult problem. For example, we know a teacher who had a personal goal of creating an informal research group with some colleagues and advanced graduate students within his department. This teacher decided that modifying his environment to create the research group would be a fruitful strategy to pursue. The project went along smoothly for several months with professors and graduate students sharing research proposals, critiquing designs, and in general contributing to each other's projects. Faculty and graduate students enjoyed the meetings and looked forward to the exchanges. Then, several months into the project, a senior faculty member began attending the sessions, and things began to change. The senior faculty member was controlling and critical of the graduate student proposals, making it seem that only her ideas were valuable; the teacher became sad and disappointed at this turn of events. When events began moving in the unanticipated direction, the teacher reviewed the strategies for achieving goals and decided to use the selecting strategy. Each time his colleague started to speak and began taking over the group, he "selected" to leave. Initially he had used the modifying strategy to realize his goal (i.e., he modified his environment to include the research group), he later used the selecting strategy as an avoidance technique (i.e., he selected to leave or walk out).

In subsequent discussions with this teacher, he became clear about his situation and the difference between using strategies to achieve goals and using them for avoidance. He refocused on achieving his goal, reviewed each strategy again, and carefully evaluated the direction in which choosing one or another would take him. In doing so, he realized that keeping the research group running was critical in achieving his long-term goal, and that his goal could not be achieved if the group disbanded. That realization led him to look at himself and the reasons he had chosen to select rather than to modify or adapt, and he realized that adapting required him to change something in himself. In this case, it required that he deal with his reluctance to confront his colleague and be honest with her about her point of view and the points of view of others in the group. Ultimately he chose to adapt by confronting her. He had to change internally by developing his courage to act in order to adapt to the change in his external environment and interact with it. His internally fearful state started to shift to a more courageous one. Although the senior faculty member said she was angry and offended, her behavior changed. In subsequent meetings, she watched and listened more often and was less critical.

## Completing Goals within a Time Frame

Goals can be distinguished from each other in terms of the amount of time you spend achieving each goal. There are short-term, intermediate, and long-term goals, but the actual time frames for short-term, intermediate, and long-term goals differ from individual to individual.

### Short-Term Goals

Short-term goals support you in achieving your intermediate goals. Many people find it reasonable to work with a six-month time period for accomplishing short-terms goals. If your time frame is too short, your goals are likely to resemble tasks and proliferate in number, making them hard to control. If your list of short-term goals becomes too lengthy, you might be working with tasks instead of short-term goals. Some examples of short-term goals that may help you see the difference between a task and a short-term goal follow. Notice that the goals are sorted into the specific domains described.

*Profession:* write a chapter in a book

*Relationships:* take a vacation with the family; participate in a monthly bridge club

*Health and fitness:* lose five pounds; run at least five times a week for 30 minutes

*Finances:* transfer my personal accounting procedures to a computer-based program

*Recreation:* learn to play "Moonlight Sonata" on the piano

*Personal education:* clear up incomplete communication with Joe

*Basic support systems:* paint the trim on the house; clean and organize the storage room

## Intermediate Goals

Intermediate goals support you in achieving your long-term goals. Intermediate goals can usually be achieved within two years. Examples of intermediate goals follow.

*Profession:* complete my master's degree in educational psychology

*Relationships:* collect information on adopting a child

*Health and fitness:* lose ten pounds; run a 10K race

*Finances:* start an educational consulting business with my colleague; start putting money in an SRA

*Recreation:* take a trip next summer just for fun

*Personal development:* complete a course in time management

*Basic support systems:* trade in my car for a later model; create a personal web page

## Long-Term Goals

Long-term goals are achieved over an extended period of time. Collectively, your long-term goals define what you want to accomplish in the longest time frame that is relevant to you. Beyond this time frame, you may not have any particular plans for your life.[7] Examples of some long-term goals that teachers have shared with us follow.

*Profession:* write a book, become the principal of a school; develop a new model for ESL instruction for my school district; finish my doctoral degree

*Relationships:* put my children through college; adopt a child

*Health and fitness:* achieve my ideal body weight; run in a half-marathon

*Finances:* create a retirement fund of $350,000; achieve a yearly income of $ _____

*Recreation:* form a rhythm and blues band and play a gig at least once a month

*Personal development:* complete at least one course in some aspect of personal development each year

*Basic support systems:* buy a new car; remodel my kitchen

## Legacy Goals

Legacy goals are different from short-term, intermediate, and long-term goals in that they are not defined in terms of the amount of time needed to achieve them. Legacy goals are the ones nearest and dearest to your heart. They define what you would like to be remembered for (if being remembered for something is important to you).[8] It is important to identify legacy goals because time spent on them will be experienced as expressing who you are and what you stand for. When you spend some time on your legacy goals, you feel like you are in touch with your heart and expressing what is most important for you.

If you would like to focus on discovering your own legacy goals, ask yourself these questions: If I knew for certain that I had only one year to live:

1. What kind of activities would be the most meaningful for me?

2. Which one or two goals would I want to accomplish?

3. What would I want to be remembered for?

Some individuals may already know what their most highly valued goals are or may find them easy to discover. Others may not have thought much about them and may need to stay with the discovery process over an extended period of time. There is no single method or single time frame that will work for everyone.

## EFFECTIVENESS ROUTINES

In addition to setting short-term, intermediate, long-term, and legacy goals, it is important to maintain a set of effectiveness routines in each domain. Effectiveness routines are regular repeated actions within a domain that are used to create and maintain an environment in which major goal-directed activities can take place. They include fulfilling regular obligations, keeping regular commitments, completing housekeeping chores, etc. Some examples of effectiveness routines that teachers have shared with us follow.

### Profession

- Keep current on email
- Reply to correspondence
- Prepare for classes
- Complete routine administrative tasks

### Relationships

- Acknowledge birthdays of my family
- Write Grandfather every week
- Call Mom every day

### Health and fitness

- Give blood every eight weeks
- Lift weights three times a week
- Swim five times a week
- Run six times a week
- Do flexibility routine seven times a week
- Do sit-ups and pushups every day
- Eat a high-protein, low-carbohydrate diet and take my supplements every day
- Walk and sit with shoulders back, eyes up

**Finances**

- Balance checkbook
- Keep tax records up to date
- Set aside money for taxes
- Pay bills

**Personal education**

- Write in a journal daily
- Read inspirational literature

**Recreation**

- Schedule free time twice a week without interference from other tasks
- Take a 30-minute nap every day

**Basic support systems**

- Time: follow monthly, weekly, and daily planning routines
- Shelter
  - Cleaning: clean home once a week
  - Repairs: fix small problems within a week of when they come up
- Clothing
  - Cleaning: wash clothes weekly and take clothes to dry cleaning every two weeks
  - Repairs: mend clothes once every month
  - Consolidation: every year, give away clothing I don't wear
- Transportation
  - Cleaning: clean car
  - Repairs: repair mechanical problems
- Communication
  - Keep up to date on correspondence
  - Return borrowed items and resolve any lost items with lenders

## DEVELOPING YOUR OWN GOALS

### *Content and Format of Goals Sheet for Each Domain*

In developing your own goals for each domain, you may find it helpful to enter information on a template as shown on pp. 126–127. The template includes the name of the domain, name of a role model, description of your ideal behaviors, a list of your legacy goal(s), short-term goals, intermediate goals, and long-term goals.

Domain:

Role Model:

Ideal Behaviors

- 
- 
- 
- 
- 
- 
- 

Legacy Goal(s)

- 
- 
- 
- 
- 
- 

Short-Term Goals (time period and date of completion)

- 
- 
- 
- 
- 
- 
-

Intermediate Goals (time period and date of completion)

- 
- 
- 
- 
- 
- 

Long-Term Goals (time period and date of completion)

- 
- 
- 
- 
- 
- 

Effectiveness Routines

- 
-

### *Process of Goal-Setting*

The same basic process can be used for developing your own goals in each domain as you used for developing your governing values. It is often useful to start by developing your long-term and legacy goals first. Then develop intermediate and short-term goals that will enable you to achieve your long-term and legacy goals. Here are some ideas that may help you in this process.

1. On a blank sheet of paper, write this question: "What goals do I want to accomplish in the long-term in a specific domain?"
2. Brainstorm
   a. Set a timer for five minutes.
   b. Write down every thought that comes to mind in response to this question.
   c. Keep your pencil (or typing fingers) moving at all times.
   d. Do not censor your thoughts in any way.
   e. Do not reject thoughts that seem to be off topic.
3. Take a break
   a. Leave the list alone for 5 to 30 minutes.
4. Consolidate
   a. Prepare a sign with the following message: "I do not have to take everything into account right now. I can keep this list and decide to focus on part of it. I can always incorporate more items at a later time. Deleting items does not mean that they are gone forever."
   b. Ask yourself this question: "If I had to focus on 5 to 15 of these goals right now, which ones would I focus on?"
   c. Take 15 minutes to reduce your list to 5 to 15 goals.

Repeat this process to develop a list of intermediate and short-term goals that will support your achieving your long-term and legacy goals in the specified domain. You will probably find it easier to take some extended time in developing your goals by coming back to them and working on them every day for a week or two rather than trying to complete the process all at one time.

In working through the process of setting goals for various domains, keep in mind that domains and goals interact; goals achieved in the domain to which you have assigned it can affect other domains as well. For example, if you have assigned your goal of changing jobs to the professional domain because the new job would be more interesting, you may find that achieving it affects the financial domain because you end up earning more money. In short, there are no hard and fast rules for assigning goals to domains.

In this chapter, our goal was to be as neutral as possible as to the relative merit of different values in order to avoid imposing our own values on others. Nonetheless, ethical considerations in defining governing values are clearly important and have been discussed extensively in the literature on ethics such as Blackburn (1999). For example, almost any ethical system that we know of emphasizes the importance of integrity and honesty. In addition to ethical considerations, psychological considerations can play an important role in defining values and setting goals. In particular, the values of inclusion, being nonjudgmental, or having respect for diversity can be particularly beneficial to the individual because they contribute to the experience of internal harmony, a topic we address in Chapter 10.[9]

## NOTES

1. We first heard about this story from a friend, George Young. We did a search on the Internet and were unable to find any single author to whom to attribute it. Moreover, it appears in a wide variety of versions.

2. In common vernacular, "where you're coming from" is used to refer to governing values, whether tacit or explicit.

3. Nonetheless, seeing how others organize their thinking about governing values or traits of highly regarded people can help us organize our own thinking. For example, Kornfeld (1994, pp. 66–78) lists the following ten qualities of what he calls "spiritual maturity," which he also characterizes as the perception of "… harmony, even amid great pain, because…(one) has found peace in…(one's)… heart": (1) nonidealism, (2) kindness, (3) patience, (4) immediacy, (5) sense of the sacred that is integrated and personal, (6) questioning, (7) flexibility, (8) embracing opposites, (9) relationship, and (10) ordinariness.

4. See Chapter 10 for a discussion of the role of projections in gossip.

5. In research design, the process of idealizing and making global judgments is called a "halo effect," which compromises the validity of one's observations and interferes with one's ability to make useful distinctions. (See Brown, 1988, p. 33.)

6. We are not likely to have a relatively complete picture of another person's life. According to Joseph Campbell, the further the story about an individual gets removed from the actual individual in space and time, the more likely it is to become a mythical account (Campbell, 1990, 1992). Trungpa (1973) further cautions that spiritual heroes can pose particular problems, particularly if you consider the person you have identified to be spiritually advanced: a guru or the like. The more strongly one holds this opinion, the more susceptible one becomes to spiritual materialism in which the image of spiritual leader and actions taken in his or her name cause more problems than the real-world issues that the person's spirituality was supposed to cure (Palmer, 1998, p. 7). Spiritual role models who actually provide good role models are very often people who do not make it a point to display their spirituality. For an extensive discussion of these issues see Kramer and Alstad, 1993.

7. There may be times in which you are not clear about your long-term goals and are searching for some sort of meaning for your life. This is normal. If you focus on short-term goals and maintenance, as well as short-term tasks that involve exploring long-term possibilities, you are eventually likely to develop your long-term goals.

8. Chris Carmichael, Lance Armstrong's training coach, characterizes the essence of dream goals (which are equivalent to legacy goals as we have defined them). "At the top end of the goal spectrum are dream goals, or ultimate goals that push the limits of possibility. Dream goals are the ones you have difficulty admitting to anyone except your closest friends. Talking about your dream goals can put you in an uncomfortable position. They are the goals that people may laugh at you for even considering. Dream goals seem worlds away when you set them, and they tend to be very inspiring." (Carmichael, 2003, pp 34–45)

9. For a discussion of a related topic, the consequences of setting goals having to do with authoritianism, control, and power, see Kramer and Alstad (1993).

# Chapter 8

# Planning to Achieve Goals

**O**nce we have developed short-term, intermediate, and long-term goals, we must turn our attention to developing a plan to achieve the goals that we have set. However, just because we have set goals does not mean that we will be successful in achieving them. We need a plan! Planning is the purposeful process of sequencing and scheduling the specific tasks required to accomplish goals.* Planning builds on the values clarification and goal-setting activities developed in Chapter 7 to ensure that daily tasks are consistent with goals and governing values.[1] Course and lesson

---

*The "purposeful" component of this definition ties it in to Sternberg's (1985) definition of intelligence. (See Chapter 7, p. 116.)

planning are essential components of teachers' lives. Even new and inexperienced teachers realize the need to think through specific steps in planning lessons. Few teachers make a habit of winging it. The same care used in lesson planning must also be applied to the overall use of time in planning for the achievement of professional and personal goals. When we use our time intelligently to accomplish goals, we experience feelings similar to what we feel when we plan a great lesson for our students.

This chapter describes four specific planning procedures that can be done yearly, monthly, weekly, or daily and a number of ideas for how you might carry them out. How often you choose to carry out the specific planning procedures is up to you as are the specific techniques you use to carry them out. We have perhaps provided more detail in this chapter than you need. Select what you find useful and what will work for you. The most important point is that carrying out deliberate planning provides maximum separation between decision-making process and the feeling of urgency to act that often arises in the context of daily activities. By separating the decision-making process from our daily tasks, we can make reasoned and purposeful decisions to use all of the executive processes in planning to achieve our goals.

## TASKS

### Definition

Central to planning is the purposeful creation of a set of specific tasks used to achieve one's goals. *Task* is a technical term we use to refer to a specific activity carried out in pursuit of an articulated goal (Bachman & Palmer, 1996).** For purposes of managing one's use of time, we restrict our definition of task to an activity that can be completed within one day.

In Figure 8.1a, the solid line between the goal and the activity indicates that the two are linked, thereby fulfilling the technical definition of a task. In Figure 8.1b, the absence of a line between a goal and the activity

---

** This is an adaptation of Bachman and Palmer's definition of task, which focuses on tasks involving language use. (See Bachman & Palmer, 1996, p. 44.)

**Figure 8.1a** Tasks

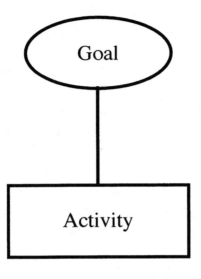

**Figure 8.1b** Activities

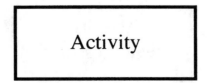

indicates that the two are not linked. Thus, the technical definition of a *task* has not been fulfilled. Figure 8.1b simply represents an activity.[2] An example of a task would be developing the first lesson for a new course (see Figure 8.2).

In relationship to planning tasks, we agree with Carroll (1993, p. 8) that it is important to know when the task has been completed. In other words, the criteria for completing the task must be specified because it can be disheartening to work on a task when the criteria for completion are not clearly specified. Not only are we unable to track our progress, we also never know when we are finished with the task. The task-planning procedures we describe are designed to meet two criteria: (1) the tasks must be clearly associated with goals on the domain/goals sheets (see p. 126), and (2) the criteria for completing each task must be clear.

### Setting Criteria for Accomplishing Tasks

Criteria for accomplishing tasks can be set in two ways: (1) results defined in terms of a specific product (e.g., copy course syllabus or register for an ESL Endorsement Program) or (2) results defined in terms of time

**Figure 8.2**   Example Task

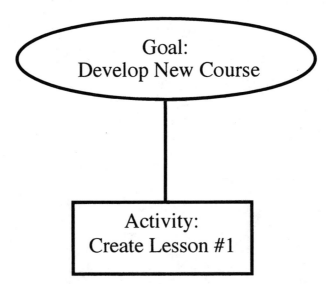

spent participating in a specific process (e.g., work on lesson plans for 1.5 hours). Setting criteria in terms of a specific product is appropriate if you believe that it is feasible for you to produce a specific product within the total amount of time allocated to the task.

Setting criteria in terms of the amount of time spent participating on a specified process is appropriate if you cannot be explicit about how much time it will take to achieve your goal or if doing so may interfere with putting in time on the task. For example, if you are writing a book, you may know that your writing process involves a certain amount of indeterminacy. On some days you may create a lot of usable text, while on other days you go around in circles. You might find that defining your writing task in terms of writing so many minutes or hours per day makes it possible for you to complete your task. You continue to put in a certain amount of time writing each day until the goal has been achieved.

### Classifying Tasks

In most systems, procedures are provided for classifying tasks by priority (i.e., how important they are). In one such system (Winwood, 1990, p. 29), "A" priority tasks are crucial, vital, or critical, and must be done. "B" priority tasks are important and should be done. "C" priority tasks are back-burner tasks and could be done. Priority-based systems like these seem to us to be somewhat limited in their usefulness because they confound two different task characteristics: (1) the value of a task and (2) the urgency of the task.

We can use the following two tasks to illustrate the difference between value and urgency—spending time with an aging parent and seeing a dentist when one has a toothache. Spending time with an aging parent probably adds a lot of value to one's life, but doing so may not be particularly urgent. It could conceivably be postponed for a short time without serious consequences. Seeing a dentist, on the other hand, might not add a lot of value to one's life but the task might be urgent. The consequence of not seeing the dentist might include a lot of pain, loss of productivity, loss of the tooth, additional medical expenses, etc.

In the chart that follows, we offer an alternative to classifying tasks by priority. Instead, we distinguish task values according to the use of individual strengths for carrying them out and characteristics of the product created.[3]

| Task Value | Use of Individual Strengths | Characteristics of the Product |
|---|---|---|
| **A-Value Tasks** Tasks that help you achieve legacy goals | + use of strengths | + progress toward accomplishing legacy goals |
| **B-Value Tasks** Productivity or work–related tasks not associated with legacy goals | ± use of strengths | + progress toward accomplishing effectiveness goals and routine tasks |
| **C-Value Tasks** Renewal/recreation tasks | + use of strengths | + progress toward accomplishing goals associated with renewal and recreation |

A-value, B-value, and C-value are defined here.

## A-Value Tasks

A-value tasks involve using individual strengths to achieve legacy goals. Recall from Chapter 6 that legacy goals are goals you would like to be remembered for, goals that help to define the best in you. For example, if your legacy goal is creating a cadre of highly competent students in a particular discipline, all tasks that you see as contributing directly toward that goal that involve using your strengths would be A-value tasks.

Using strengths in this process draws on specialties as described in Chapter 6. For example, if we have an Adapted Child specialty (i.e., *Sensitive*), executing A-value tasks would involve using our sensitivity. If we have a Critical Parent specialty (i.e., *Influential*), executing A-value tasks might involve influencing others. In addition to focusing on the use of strengths, A-value tasks also involve making progress toward a particular product (i.e., accomplishing legacy goals).

Executing A-value tasks involves experiencing work as play, and participating in these tasks evokes a particularly strong sense that we are living our particular version of a meaningful life. A-value tasks resonate with our spirit. For example, in talking about learning to work on guitar amplifiers, Terry Dobbs (2002, p. 10) said, "I rounded up all of the electronics books I could find—tube books, solid state—it was a painstaking process, but when you have a passion for something, it really doesn't feel like work." When we plan for the use of time, it is important to spend some time working on A-value tasks regardless of what other demands there may be on your time, even if the A-value tasks do not seem urgent. (A-value tasks may not seem urgent since they are often related to long-term goals.) However, time spent on A-value tasks during periods of high levels of activity provides experiential reference points by which to assess the overall balance of tasks in your daily life.

## B-Value Tasks

B-value tasks are important and often necessary, but they are not associated with achieving legacy goals. They are often required to create and maintain basic support systems. B-value tasks may take much of your time, but they should not take all of it. B-value tasks should operate in the background to make your life work well enough to let you do A-value tasks. Because the processes may not always be enjoyable, B-value tasks are often perceived as "work." They are generally associated with effectiveness and routine tasks that are necessary to make our lives work. Also, B-value tasks may not involve using strengths. For example, a teacher might not particularly enjoy organizing her office environment or be very good at it, yet she could still realize that time spent organizing is important if she wants to find things in a timely manner and maintain an efficient and productive work life.

## C-Value Tasks

C-value tasks are associated with goals involving renewal (see Merton, 1999), recreation, or play and are not directly associated with goals in other domains. C-value tasks are highly enjoyable and/or relaxing in and of themselves. They can include recreational activities such as playing sports, going to movies, watching TV, recreational eating, listening to music, listening to the radio, etc., as well as resting. For example, if you enjoy listening to music and do so for sheer enjoyment, listening to music would be a C-value task. C-value tasks are needed for renewal and maintaining energy levels on A-value and B-value tasks, and they generally make use of our strengths. For example, if going to sentimental movies is renewing for you, the ability to appreciate such movies might draw on your emotional sensitivity (associated with the Adapted Child perspective).

It is important to point out that in general there is nothing inherent in a task that automatically places it into an A, B, or C category. Placement of a task in a category is a result of the purpose you assign to the task and your own experience of the process of executing it. For example, if you enjoy listening to music and do so for sheer enjoyment, it is a C-value task. If you enjoy listening to music and do so for use in creating a language teaching course that is near and dear to your heart, then listening to music can move up to an A-value task. If you decide you need to listen to music in order to prepare a lesson plan for a course you are teaching, then doing so becomes a B-value task. Thus, what might be a C-value task for one person might be an A-value task for another one. We now turn to one type of activity that does not fall within the A, B, and C categories we use to assign value to tasks.

## Type-1 Activities

Some activities take up time in our lives, but they are not tasks because they are not attached to goals. Such activities sometimes involve doing something you do not want to do out of fear of saying no to someone or looking bad in the eyes of others. We call these Type-1 activities. Participating in these activities often involves a certain amount of dishonesty with one's self or others (e.g., I may do the activity, but I won't tell you that I don't want to do it).

Continually participating in Type-1 activities over the long haul damages our self-concept and reinforces our self-doubts. For example, suppose a colleague asks you to help him organize his files because he knows that you are good at it. You do not want to spend your time doing this, yet you are afraid that you will appear selfish if you do not agree to help out. If you agree to help out anyway, you may reinforce your self-doubt (i.e., "I'm really selfish because I didn't want to help, and it's somehow bad to be selfish. I don't want to acknowledge or accept this selfish aspect of myself."). Moreover, when you do this frequently, you may also lose track of your own governing values and goals and the opportunity to incorporate them in your decision-making. Thus the value of Type-1 activities is negative. Nonetheless, we include Type-1 activities in the planning process because participating in them takes time and energy, and being aware of the amount of time we may be spending on such activities is an important component in monitoring how we plan. Mostly likely, a few Type-1 activities are to be expected in anyone's life. However, if you find you are spending too much time on Type-1 activities, examine the circumstances in which you commit to them.***

## TIME FOR PLANNING

Intelligent planning requires both an interval of time for planning and a schedule that allows you to separate the planning time from the time at which you will take action on your plan. If you are not busy, it may seem fairly easy to take the time necessary to develop and use an efficient planning procedure. If you are busy, you may feel like you just don't have enough time to plan. If this is the case, it may take a particular act of will to set aside the time for planning, It may also take an overdose of the downside of excessive busyness (e.g., exhaustion, inability to keep overextended agreements, health problems, inability to achieve other goals in your life, etc.) to bring you to the point of taking time out from your busy day to plan ways to get your life under control.[4]

In the final part of this chapter, we turn to some actual procedures for generating tasks consistent with one's goals and values and assigning them to particular times. In describing these procedures, we try as much as we can to focus on general principles and leave many of the mechanical details to the particular system (computer-based, pencil-and-paper-based) up to you. In general, planning moves in stages from yearly to daily planning sessions. The number of stages you ultimately decide to use between yearly and daily planning is up to you. Examples of yearly, monthly, and weekly planning follow.[5]

---

***See the discussion of the *Helpful* and *Sensitive* specialties in overuse in Chapter 6.

## YEARLY PLANNING

Yearly planning sessions are used to take stock of your entire set of governing values and goals, revise them if necessary, and set target dates for completion of your goals. Many teachers like to do their yearly planning just before the New Year as a kind of formalized opportunity to make New Year's resolutions. Others prefer vacation times, when they may feel more relaxed and are out from under the pressures of the daily routine. Whatever time you choose, it is important that enough time be set aside.

These steps in yearly planning procedures assume that you have already created a list of your governing values and goals in your planning procedures (see Chapter 7).

1. Reflect on and revise your governing values as needed.
2. Reflect on what you have accomplished during the preceding year in terms of accomplishing your goals in each domain.
   a. How much time have you put in and what progress have you made on your legacy goals?
   b. Where have selection, modification, and adaptation strategies been most effective in allowing you to accomplish your goals?
3. Revise your domain/goals sheets as needed (see pp. 126–127 in Chapter 7). Much of the information will remain stable after you have had some experience with planning.
4. Put specific completion dates next to your long-term, intermediate, and short-term goals. After you have carried out your first yearly planning session, try to leave your long-term goal target dates the same for several years so the dates do not move ahead one year every year.

## MONTHLY PLANNING

Monthly planning sessions are used to decide what goals are important for you to put time in during the upcoming month.

1. Prioritize your domain/goal sheets (see pages 126–127 in Chapter 7) in the order of their importance to you in the upcoming month. It is normal for certain areas of our lives to be more important to us at one time than another. One easy way to do this is by printing out the goals and values sheets and putting them in a notebook in the order of their importance. This provides a physical means of recognizing this ordering. You can accomplish the same thing by cutting and pasting pages in a word processing document.

2. Identify the specific short-term and legacy goals in each domain on which you plan to devote time during the month. Be sure to include legacy goals in this process. Then highlight the specific goals on which you plan to spend time during the month.[6] For example, suppose one of your short-term goals is preparing a presentation for a professional conference, but you prefer to spend time on this preparation during a break in your teaching schedule. You may decide that the month ahead is not a good time to prepare for the conference, so you would not highlight this particular goal for the upcoming month.

3. When you have completed your monthly planning, look at your domain/goals sheets: the order in which they occur reflects their relative importance to you for the upcoming month, and the highlighted goals in each sheet identify the specific goals on which you plan to spend time.

## PLANNING FOR THE WEEK
## (CARRIED OUT IN A SINGLE PLANNING SESSION)

Weekly and daily planning actually take place *during a single session* at weekly (not daily) intervals (such as every Sunday evening). The purpose of this planning is to reflect deliberately on how you plan to spend your time during the week as a whole and during each day of the week. The result of these planning sessions will consist of a set of prioritized tasks that you plan to complete each day of the week. Time spent on advanced weekly and daily planning takes the place of much of the time you would spend in planning before the start of each day (if you actually take time out to plan your day). Advanced weekly and daily planning only takes a few minutes each week once you get the hang of it. Moreover, once you get in the habit of doing it you may find that you enjoy it. For ease of presentation, we will describe the weekly and daily components of the weekly and daily planning separately, even though they take place during a single planning session.

### Materials and Equipment Used for Weekly Planning

If you have never done weekly planning before or if you feel that your own system for planning could use some help, you might try this procedure. Many people find the process that we describe to be very helpful. To prepare for your weekly planning, you will need copies of your domain/goals sheets (which you created during your monthly planning session), as well as a separate blank sheet of paper for each domain/goals sheet. Pages 144–145 provide an example of the two sheets used for weekly planning. The right-hand page column contains your values and goals in the Intellectual and Professional domain. The left-hand page is used to record specific tasks in the Intellectual and Professional domain that you are considering executing during the next week.

### Steps in Weekly Planning

### Step 1: Decide which goals you want to put time into during the week

Look at your highlighted legacy and short-term goals for the month. Think about which of these goals you want to put time in on *during the current week*. When you decide that you want to put time in on a specific legacy or short-term goal, indicate this by putting a tick next to the goal.

### Step 2: Preliminary task development

The purpose of preliminary task development is to prepare a list of specific tasks that will allow you to make progress toward meeting your goals during the week. Each of these tasks should be completed in one day. Tasks that might appear to be stretched out over several days can be thought of as a series of repeated daily tasks. Again, the purpose of thinking of tasks in this way is to be able to distinguish between tasks and goals. Brainstorm a list of specific tasks that you think you could do in the following week that would move you on your path toward achieving each identified goal (marked with a tick). Copy the tasks on the sheet of paper designated for tasks.

### *Materials and Equipment used in Daily Planning*

To carry out daily planning, you will need daily planning forms such as a calendar, a small notebook, a commercial paper-and-pencil day-planning system, or a handheld electronic planner (probably used in conjunction with a personal computer). Whatever type of daily planning form you use, you will need a way to note the following for each day:

1. Task description
2. Task value: A, B, or C
3. Commitment index: + or − (see discussion on p. 146)
4. Status: whether the task has been completed or has been deleted
5. Times for appointments

Most commercially available paper or computer-based systems include the components in this list, even though these components may not be labeled exactly as they are in this sample.

### *Steps in Advanced Daily Planning*

#### Step 1: Enter tasks on a daily task list or in an appointment book.

The purpose of entering tasks on daily task lists is to think through and decide which tasks will be accomplished on each day of the week. You want to schedule a reasonable number of tasks that you can realistically execute. Transfer the tasks you have brainstormed for the week to your planning system so you can see when to execute each task. Remember that appointments and meetings are also tasks.

## PROFESSIONAL
## TASKS

### (Week of March 1–7, 2007)

- 
- 
- 
- 
- 
- 
-

# DOMAIN:
# PROFESSION
## (March 2007)

Role model: Earl Stevick

Ideal behaviors

- I am a productive and efficient writer.
- I conduct careful and thoughtful research.
- I prepare carefully and completely for my classes.

Legacy goals

- Publish series for young learners.
- Get elected to the TESOL board.

Short-term goals (6 months)

- Finish the draft scope and sequence for Book 1 in series for young learners.
- Prepare lectures for new methods course.
- Audit Arabic 101 at least 3 times a week for six months.
- Prepare professional resume.

Intermediate goals (1 year)

- Find a publisher for series for young learners.
- Teach new methods course.
- Get to an intermediate stage in spoken Arabic.

Long-term goals (5 years)

- Get promoted to associate professor.

Effectiveness routines

- Clear E-mail.
- Organize files and bookshelves.
- Reply to correspondence.
- Prepare for classes.

### Step 2: Enter the value of the tasks

The purpose of entering the value of tasks is to allow you to determine at a glance the value of contribution (A, B, or C) that each task makes to your goals. Write the value (A, B, or C) adjacent to the task (or appointment).

### Step 3: Establish commitment index

The purpose of the commitment index is to determine your level of determination to complete each task. The index consists of two values: committed or optional. In a paper-and-pencil system, record the commitment index (+ or -) next to the task's value.

### Step 4: Check feasibility

The purpose of the feasibility check is to determine whether your projected daily plans can be completed in the available time while also providing you with time for renewal and reflection on what you have accomplished. Ask yourself whether you will have time to complete all of the tasks and also keep appointments you have tentatively scheduled for each day. Think about the approximate time needed to complete each task. If you do not think you have sufficient time to complete all tasks, remove a task and make a decision about when to schedule this task in the future.

Part of the value in taking time to do a feasibility check is that it requires you to slow down. If you are too busy to follow the procedure, you may have too much activity in your life and you may be setting yourself up to be less effective than you are capable of being.

### Step 5: Make final value check

The purpose of the final value check is to determine whether the overall value of your tasks each day is consistent with your goals. Examine the balance of A, B, and C value tasks and Type-1 activities during the week. Have you included sufficient A-value tasks so that you are making progress toward the goals that are most important to you? Have you included enough B-value tasks to keep up with work and maintenance activities? Have you included enough C-value tasks to keep you from getting burned out? How much time do you spend on Type-1 activities?[7]

## Step 6: Do other planning

The purpose of other planning is to review your daily task/appointment lists for the upcoming week to determine whether you have included important effectiveness tasks such as class preparations, deadlines, and commitments that will be due during the week. Having done so, add the appropriate tasks for keeping these commitments to the appropriate daily task lists for the week (see the section that follows) with enough lead-time for you to feel that you are ahead of those deadlines.

## *Daily Planning*

The purpose of final daily planning is to take care of things that come up at the last minute: requests from family and colleagues, duties assigned at the last moment, emergencies such as the car problems, invitations from friends, etc. Daily planning can be carried out in the evening prior to the day being planned or first thing in the morning. It should take no more than ten minutes and should be done when you are alone, not distracted, and not in a hurry since trying to rush the process prevents you from making your best decisions. With proactive (monthly, weekly, and daily) planning, last-minute tasks and appointments that come up during final daily planning can be evaluated in the context of a predetermined plan and you can avoid the tyranny of the urgent (Mackenzie, 1997).

For example, if a student makes a last-minute request for you to read over and comment on a paper or a colleague needs a copy of a paper that he did not keep track of and asks you to stop everything and get your copy for him, you have a basis for turning this down if the time involved would take you away from your plan for the day. In your mind, you can say to yourself, "Let me see what I have already planned for today" and examine the impact of saying yes to the request. With planning of this sort, you may find yourself saying no more often, but you will experience less stress with fewer unplanned tasks. If you feel under pressure to add tasks to your list, do your best to resist this pressure and focus on allowing yourself time to experience the satisfaction you get from accomplishing what you have planned. During your final daily planning, you can also make a final check on tasks to see whether the number of items on the list is realistic given the amount of time and energy you have available. This is very important, particularly for people who tend to over-commit themselves. Reflect on or assess what you have created and ask yourself whether you have enough time and energy to complete all of the "+ commitment" tasks on your list.

## CHANGING THE EXTENT OF PLANNING

During certain stages of your career, you may find that using a systematic planning procedure every day helps you clarify what kinds of tasks you need to perform in order to experience your use of time as pleasant, satisfying, or privileged. At other times, you may already have a clear sense of your goals and the kinds of tasks needed to accomplish them and need little formal planning to incorporate them in your daily routine. In short, there is no single correct way to plan; there are only alternatives. Planning is not about creating more work for yourself. It's also not just about managing your time, although this is important. We think that the process of planning to achieve goals and ultimately executing your plan is ultimately more about getting to know yourself than about imposing a lifetime of structure on your use of time.

## NOTES

1. Although planning clearly incorporates and builds on goals, we believe it is possible to set goals without planning one's use of time to achieve these goals, and it is also possible to plan one's use of time without having a clear idea of one's goals in mind. We do not use planning in these senses in this book.

2. Activities include a very wide range of behaviors and can surely be classified in many ways. For example, behaviors could be classified in terms of whether they are consistent or inconsistent with one's governing values (i.e., in or out of one's integrity), or they could be classified in terms of whether or not they are emotion-driven. A discussion of types of behaviors would be wide ranging and beyond the scope of this book.

3. Many time management systems, such as task lists in the Palm™ desktop, provide mechanisms for labeling tasks according to both category and priority.

What we have done here is try to clarify the characteristics one might use to assign different task value labels.

4. Emotional hijacking can also interfere with the ability to create intelligent goals and plans. When you have a lot of seemingly urgent tasks on your mind and attempt to plan your use of time, you will not have the resources (blood supply to the cerebral cortex) to make well-thought-out decisions. Your attempts at time management will evolve into writing down a list of tasks that seem urgent (emotionally charged) at the moment—this urgency is created again by the dominating control of the emotions. So whatever plans you may make will not reflect your governing values, your long-term goals, and your ability to intelligently decide on alternative courses of action (adapting to, modifying, or selecting your environment in harmony with your goals and abilities).

5. When we suggest that teachers consider devoting some time to planning their use of time, we frequently hear that they do not have enough time to do so or that it seems too complicated. Some teachers raising this objection actually enjoy being as busy as they are and feel like they are spending their time exactly as they like to. If they do not complain about it or in other ways act out their dissatisfaction, then there is probably no reason for them to spend extra time on planning. However, other teachers are busier than they indicate they would like to be. These teachers seem to be in a double bind. They are busier than they want to be and dissatisfied with the way they spend their time, but this very busyness is used as an excuse for not doing anything about it. They ultimately paint themselves as victims, and as we have seen, specialties in overuse (such as Victim) are often experienced to be inescapable characteristics of who we are. In talking with these teachers, we try to lay out characteristics of their specialties in a nonjudgmental way and then leave it up to them do something about them or not. We also try our best not to participate in conversations in which we commiserate with them about their busyness, which would tend to reinforce the seeming lack of choice that the specialty in overuse creates.

6. If you are not working with printed domain/goals sheets, find some other way to identify the specific goals you plan to spend time on during the month.

7. Be sure that even if your current occupation might be very unsatisfying at the moment, you are still putting time in toward moving toward highly valued goals.

"You are satisfied when you accomplish your goal, but then again, when you start reflecting on how you accomplished it, you start seeing how you could have been a little better."

Tiger Woods
*The Oprah Winfrey Show*
(2001)

# Chapter 9

# Implementation and Evaluation

No matter how well intentioned we are or how clear and purposeful we are in the process of clarifying values, setting goals, and planning to achieve goals, our efforts will be futile if we do not commit to the implementation of goals and the evaluation of our plan. The processes we describe in this chapter are iterative (i.e., done over and over again) rather than linear (i.e., done only one time). There are, in general, two phases to this process. The first phase in implementing your plan is what we call the *control phase*. The focus in this phase is to establish initial control in your life. Control principally occurs as a result of doing tasks. It is through doing tasks that you learn your limitations and more about the parameters of your own comfort zone. It is important to become aware of these parameters to know when to relax and when to push yourself beyond the boundaries of your comfort zone. The second phase is called the *maintenance phase.* In this phase the focus is on maintaining the processes that work for you in implementation and evaluation. However, it is not necessarily the case that one can reach the maintenance phase quickly. It often takes time and commitment to get to the phase where your focus is on maintaining rather than on establishing control. Chapter 9 focuses on how to establish control in the implementation and evaluation process so that you can eventually move into the maintenance phase.

## IMPLEMENTATION

Chapter 8 focused on developing a plan for achieving goals. Once you do this, it is important to do your best to follow the plan that you develop. However, following a plan is not without its challenges. Perhaps the biggest challenge lies in completing all of the tasks in the plan or all of the tasks on your daily list. At least initially, it is imperative to complete all of the A-value tasks and, in addition, try to complete the other tasks to which you have committed. However, this is not always easy because developing a sense of how many tasks can be completed within a certain time frame takes practice, and it is only through completing tasks that we develop this sense of task in relationship to time.

Another challenge rests with not adding any tasks to your list during the day. Although we recognize that keeping the list of tasks static is not always possible, we believe that it is important to make an attempt to do so because adding tasks to your daily lists consistently undermines the planning process itself (tasks added under pressure are not subject to planning as we have described it).

A third challenge rests in not adding time to your tasks just to complete them. Resisting the temptation to add 30 minutes or an hour to the time planned for a task in order to complete it is difficult, but leaving tasks unfinished will also tell you something about the efficacy of your plan. Executing your plan by completing all tasks, by not adding tasks to your daily list, and by not adding time to your tasks will provide you with a baseline experience of the process and also give you insight into your behavior relative to the process.

When you take time to plan intelligently and attempt to carry out your plan, your decisions are not subject to emotional hijacking or habitual ways of reacting; moreover, following your plan will enable you to learn something about planning itself. When you actually follow your plan, you collect the information necessary to reflect on the experiential consequences of having followed your plan. If you do not follow your plan, you will not be able to reflect on the consequences of your planning. You will have no experience of the consequences of your planning and, therefore, no basis for making changes in your planning and in your life.

If you are new to planning and executing tasks in your plan, keep the process of following your plan from becoming too onerous; try out your plan for a few days with the intent of reflecting on your experience and making necessary changes. As previously mentioned, it takes practice to know how many tasks to include in your plan and how long it will take to complete each task. In your evaluation, focus on the pros and cons of sticking to this plan. You do not want to feel like you have locked yourself in a room with no windows. Keep in mind that planning is not about being rigid in your life; it is about making your life more enjoyable and easier to appreciate. Determining how flexible to be with your planning develops through the experience of committing to the plan that you make and reflecting on the consequences. The effectiveness of the planning is evidenced in how well and consistently you are able to implement what you have planned.

### Ordering of Tasks

If possible, start working on your A-value tasks first. This procedure for completing tasks sets a context for the rest of the B- and C-value tasks that you wish to complete. Executing your plan by beginning with A-value tasks ensures that at least some of your time during the day will be spent on tasks that are near and dear to your heart.

For example, for a number of years Christison got up one hour earlier in the morning in order to have time to work on things that were most important to her (i.e., A-level tasks), such as writing and creating materials for books and doing her research. She knew if she did not find time for A-level activities, she would not be happy over the long term.

## Task Completion

As soon as you have completed a task, take time to check it off your list immediately. Do not start on another task and leave checking off the prior task until later. The checking-off process may seem like a small thing, but checking off tasks when they have been completed is an important motivator for participating in the process. In addition, taking a few moments after you have completed a task to do nothing is another important motivator. Experience the feeling of completion by giving yourself a minute or two of quiet relaxation to slow down before starting another task.

## Dealing with Resistance

During the day, you may realize that you are resisting working on a required task. You may find yourself contemplating changing the value or priority of the task, deleting it, or moving it to another day. This resistance is normal, and almost everyone experiences it at one point or another. One helpful way of thinking about resistance is to consider it as an instance of a conflict between two internal perspectives: One perspective wants to complete the task, and the other perspective does not. In Chapter 10, we introduce some procedures for working with conflicting internal perspectives.

## Dealing with Adding and Deleting Tasks

During the day, you may realize that you are feeling pressure to add or delete tasks from your list. Both processes involve making a change to your plan, and there are many reasons why we feel such pressures. Here are a few of the reasons that have come up for us regarding adding and deleting tasks.

*Reasons for adding tasks*

1. I have extra time, I feel energetic, and I can get ahead on my B-value tasks.

2. I have extra time, it would be fun to do such and such, and so I'll add a C-value task.

3. I forgot that I needed to do a required task.

4. I was just given this task because someone else did not plan well. I couldn't have planned for this task. And it's urgent for the other person and perhaps for me, too.

5. I know better now.

6. I didn't take time to plan well.

7. This is beyond planning.

*Reasons for deleting tasks*

1. I don't have time to complete the task because it took longer than anticipated to complete another task.

2. The task was optional in my plan.

3. I simply don't want to do it.

4. I didn't take time to plan well. I now see that I don't need to do it. It's not so important.

Of course, these lists are not meant to be exhaustive, but they do offer examples that need to be considered from two different positions—the internal perspective conflict (which we mentioned will be addressed in Chapter 10) and the specialty in overuse. How you deal with the reasons for adding to or deleting tasks from the list often involves one or the other of these components of the internal world.

The reasons you may have for adding tasks to a list could trigger a specialty in overuse. For example, suppose a student comes in who has put off registering for his classes, knowing full well that there was a deadline for doing so. (This is an example of #4 in the Reasons for adding tasks list.) Of course, the student feels that he absolutely must see you immediately to plead his case and get you involved in helping make a case with the administration. If you have the specialty *Helpful*, you may feel it is your responsibility to assist the student, and you may feel a very strong emotional push to do so. You might resolve this situation for yourself by talking with a colleague who does not have the specialty *Helpful*. Ask her how she would proceed, and consider taking the colleague's advice. Even if you don't take your colleague's advice, you at least have a clearer understanding of how your specialty may be influencing your decision to add an extra task to your list.

Reasons for deleting tasks from lists should also undergo careful scrutiny. For example, let's consider reason #3 for deleting tasks on the list: "I simply don't want to do it." Most of us can resonate with this reason for wishing to delete a task. We planned for the task, and it needs to be done; however, when it comes time to do it, we simply do not want to do it. Before deleting a task, it is important to remember that we created our daily prioritized task list when we had ample time to use our executive processes to guide us, and during this process, we clearly recognized the need to complete the task. However, at the moment of implementation, the decision-making process is always subject to emotional hijacking. It is risky to rely on decisions made during these times.

There is no right or wrong answer to the question of whether to add or delete tasks from your list, as there are probably good reasons both for doing so and not doing so. The main point is to consider the tasks and our reasons carefully before adding or deleting them, knowing that the motivation may involve a specialty in overuse, emotional hijacking, or an internal perspective conflict. Any one of these reasons can keep us from making reasoned and well-thought-out decisions.

## TRACKING PROGRESS ON TASKS

Tracking is the process of recording the progress you have made on the tasks in your prioritized daily task list. This includes identifying tasks that have been completed and also keeping track of incomplete tasks. Since completing all tasks within the allotted time frame is difficult even for the most experienced planners, we need some way of tracking incomplete tasks so that the information does not get lost and that these tasks eventually get rescheduled and completed. To keep track of progress, you will need a set of convenient symbols. The following is one possible set used in the Franklin time management system (Winwood, 1990), which we have found useful. You can use a system along these lines if you use a pencil-and-paper system, or you can find or develop alternatives that perform the same functions in electronic time management systems.

| Tracking symbols | | |
|---|---|---|
| √ | = | task completed |
| • | = | task started and in progress |
| → | = | task moved forward to a future daily task list |
| x | = | task deleted |

## EVALUATION

Evaluation involves setting time aside to assess past events and put them in perspective,[*] and it is best accomplished when you can devote your full attention to what you are evaluating. We believe evaluation consists of two components: reflecting on the intelligence of your plan and reflecting on the implementation of your plan.[1]

### Evaluating the Intelligence of Your Plan

Evaluating the intelligence of your plan involves taking stock of the relationship between what you planned to do and what you actually did. It involves not only what you accomplished but how you accomplished them. Focusing on how you accomplished your plan provides you with an opportunity to evaluate the intelligence (using Sternberg's definition) of your overall plan by looking at the results of your choice of strategies for accomplishing your goals: selecting among environments, modifying environments, or adapting to environments.

---

[*]See Sprinthall and Sprinthall (1990, pp. 21, 417) for a different approach to evaluation.

A specific set of questions to guide your evaluation process follows. We also offer extended examples for each question to provide clarification for the question and to situate it within a context. To illustrate the points, we have focused the extended examples on scenarios wherein selected strategies did not work well. The questions are intended to help you reflect on the intelligence of your plan while keeping in mind your governing values and goals, particularly your legacy goals.

1. Did your plan involve taking on tasks that created resistance to your environment (i.e., taking on a fight that would better have been avoided)? If yes, where? Another way to ask this questions is, "Did you pick your battles well?" Would it have been more intelligent to use another strategy (i.e., to select by avoiding the situation or by adapting to it)?

Extended example: Teacher A committed to completing a project hoping that Teacher B would help her. After Teacher A committed to this project, she approached Teacher B asking for *his* help. Teacher B reminded Teacher A of a previous conversation between the two of them wherein Teacher B had outlined how busy he was and in which he had decided not to commit himself to taking on anymore tasks. Teacher A felt angry with Teacher B, stating that she would not have taken on the project had she known that she could not count on her friend, Teacher B, to help her. (She somehow felt that she was entitled to Teacher B's help.) Teacher A spent considerable time and energy trying to talk Teacher B into changing *his* mind (i.e., she spent time trying to modify her environment). However, Teacher B held to his decision. Teacher A wasted important resources and pushed an important friendship very close to destruction by trying to convince Teacher B to help her. In this situation, it would have been more intelligent for Teacher A to either select a different environment (e.g., try to find another teacher to help) or adapt to her environment rather than to try to modify it.

2. In the implementation of your plan, did you give in to your environment unnecessarily? If yes, where?

Extended example: Professor A works in a university academic department that is having some troubles financially. Because of Professor A's skills in financial management, he is asked to become the new department chair, a position he has clearly expressed no interest in previously. While he is good at financial management and balancing and tracking budgets, he does not particularly like to solve department-level problems, attend meetings, do strategic planning, or work closely with colleagues in other departments. He wants to teach his small graduate classes, conduct his research, and go home. Nevertheless, because of pressure from his colleagues and their flattering comments, he accepts the position. He selects an environment (department chair) that is not consistent with his interests and goals. In this situation, it would have been more intelligent for Professor A to have maintained the status quo in his environment (i.e., maintained his previous selection) in order to accomplish his goals of teaching and conducting research.

3. Did you experience emotional hijacking, letting fear or other emotions motivate your behavior rather than your governing values? If yes, when?

Extended example: Student A has "being honest and communicating openly" as a governing value. He is working on a project with two other students. Each person in the group has taken the responsibility for one piece of the project and agreed on a deadline for completion. The group agrees to meet on the day of its self-imposed deadline to review each other's work and develop a plan to complete their project by the deadline for the course. Student A and Student B complete their work by their group deadline, but Student C does not. In fact, she admits she has not even started the project. Although Student A has "being honest and communicating openly" as a governing value, he says nothing to Student C about her failure to meet the self-imposed deadline because he fears having a confrontation with his peer. In addition, Student A becomes so upset that he is unable to talk rationally about the issues to Student C, so the group accomplishes nothing at the meeting, everyone leaves upset, and no one has a clear direction of what to do to complete the process. Student A's failure to communicate is a result of emotional hijacking.

4. In the execution of your plan to accomplish your goal, did you select inappropriately from among your environments? If yes, when? Would it have been more intelligent to use another process, such as avoiding the situation or responding in a different way?

<u>Extended example</u>: Teacher A works with Supervisor B. Supervisor B struggles with managing time; he also has a short temper, and he blames others for problems that often begin with him. On the other hand, Supervisor A works very hard and spends an enormous amount of time and energy devoted to his work and the success of the program. Teacher A is aware of the strengths and weaknesses of Supervisor B. Teacher A has worked for the school district in question for only one year, so she has no seniority and few connections. Supervisor B has given Teacher A the task of reworking the history curriculum for her school but she is given no deadlines by her supervisor. Hoping that she has plenty of time, Teacher A establishes a timeline for revising the curriculum that works for her and allows her time to make revisions and get feedback from her peers. One Monday morning, Teacher A is told by Supervisor B that he needs the revised curriculum the next day. Teacher A gets defensive, blaming Supervisor B for not giving her a deadline. Supervisor B gets angry and blames Teacher A for not getting the curriculum revised. Supervisor B gives Teacher A a bad report on her end-of-semester review.

In this case, Teacher A was aware of the particular weakness of Supervisor B (his inability to manage time), but Teacher A did not take this into account. She used the selection process (and, in effect, selected an environment to work in that didn't exist—i.e., one in which she could count on her supervisor to be organized). A more intelligent process would have been to adapt to the environment as it really was and adjust to her supervisor's known lack of ability to manage his time.

5. In the implementation of your plan, did you inappropriately try to modify your environment? If yes, when?

<u>Extended example</u>: Professor A has been teaching a methodology class for several years, and he has spent an enormous amount of time and energy developing the course. Without consulting him, the depart-

ment chair assigns the course to a new adjunct faculty member to teach and gives Professor A a new course that will require an enormous amount of new preparation. The department chair says that there is no one else on the faculty who can teach the new course and that the adjunct faculty member has had previous experience with L2 methodology courses. The department chair's reason for making this decision was that she believed it was in the best interests of the Department. Professor A has approximately four months to prepare for the course.

Professor A decides to resist the department chair's assignment and tries to modify his environment by putting a huge amount of effort into trying to get the department chair to change her mind and even goes to the dean to try to get his way. After three months, it becomes clear that Professor A will have to teach the new course and now has only one month to prepare. On reflection, it becomes clear to Professor A that his use of the modification process was not an intelligent course of action. If he had adapted to the environment in which he was working (including his department chair), he would have had four months to prepare. He might also have come to the realization that the department chair was doing the best she could with limited resources.

The chart below may be useful in systematically reflecting and assessing the intelligent use of your plan.

| Task Number | Intelligently Executed | Unintelligent Selection | Unintelligent Adaptation | Unintelligent Modification |
|---|---|---|---|---|
| Task 1 | | | | |
| Task 2 | | | | |
| Task 3 | | | | |
| etc. | | | | |

## Implementing Your Plan

If you executed or accomplished just what you planned for, you do not need to evaluate the general process of implementing your plan. If you did not execute your plan as outlined, you either accomplished more than you planned for (you added tasks to your plan), or you accomplished less than you planned for (you deleted tasks from your plan or moved them to a future date.). While there is nothing wrong with either of these implementation strategies, if you find yourself consistently using one or the other, systematic evaluation will help you determine the possible causes and come up with an appropriate course of action to deal with these causes.

## Accomplishing More than You Planned

If you consistently add tasks to your list and think of yourself as an overachiever, you may find that the more you get ahead, the further the road in front of you extends. It may appear to you that since you have no stable goal or finish line, you never get there. You may also find that your life is always busy. In addition, you may also deny yourself the down time that you need to experience the satisfaction of what you have accomplished, and you may begin to experience some of the problems that being excessively busy can create: excessive stress and the familiar medical and emotional problems that accompany long-term stress.

To become aware of why you add tasks to your day, you can reflect on the ways that you justify these additions. While some justifications for adding tasks are genuinely worth taking seriously, many others are not. Some justifications only seem to be urgent because they are being considered in the urgency of the moment rather than in a planning process that involves the use of the executive processes. Reflecting on the justifications for adding tasks at a time when you have little emotional involvement or feeling of urgency about the tasks can provide you with useful insight about the underlying reasons. To structure reflection of this type, write down your justifications for adding each task to your list and the negative consequences that may have resulted from not having added the task to the list. We have found this chart useful.

| Added Tasks | Justifications | Negative Consequences (on Reflection) of Not Adding the Task |
|---|---|---|
| Added task #1 | | |
| Added task #2 | | |
| Added task #3 | | |
| Added task #4 | | |

Some other questions to ask about adding tasks include:

1. Were my reactions congruent with my governing values?
2. Were my reactions congruent with my goals, particularly my legacy goals?
3. Would I have planned to add this task if I had known about it beforehand and during planning time?
4. Were reactions that lead to adding the task part of a specialty in overuse?

If you tend to fill your time executing not-planned-for tasks, you may notice that the moment an idea such as answering mail, ordering a book, making a phone call, cleaning, etc., occurs to you, it dominates your thoughts, and it seems as if doing it now will satisfy you. Momentary gratification of this type is unlike the satisfaction that results from doing planned tasks. If an idea about adding a task is important, it can always go into a prioritized daily task list for some future day. Placing ideas for tasks on a future task list means that the task can be evaluated for inclusion during the planning session and, then, can be carried out in a systematic way. Having a system for responding to impulsive tasks may be all that is needed to help dispel the urge to do them immediately and may help you relax about not doing the task right away. Without breaking the connection between the thought and the action, we continue to respond and make life busier and less satisfying than it should be.

Finally, we would like to emphasize that accomplishing more than what you planned for is not necessarily a problem. It may simply indicate that you are learning that you can comfortably do more than you are accustomed to thinking you can do. Over time, you will be able to revise your plan so that you make this accommodation.

## Accomplishing Less than What You Planned

There are a number of reasons why you may not complete all of your planned-for tasks on your prioritized daily task list. One possibility is that your plan itself was unrealistic. If this is the case, the process of completing everything on your list for a limited period of time, particularly if this means staying up late to do so and feeling exhausted, will quickly teach you how to plan more intelligently.

Another possibility is that your plan was fine; it represented an intelligently balanced set of tasks for accomplishing your goals that are consistent with your governing values. It may also mean that you had the resources for completing all of the planned-for tasks. However, for one reason or another, you put off completing some of the tasks or were not able to finish the tasks in the time allocated. There are surely many possible causes for not completing tasks (for example, not eating well enough to maintain your energy levels), and investigating all of these causes clearly goes far beyond the scope of this chapter. Therefore, we have opted to present three strategies that we have found the most useful in helping us complete tasks on our daily plan and, thereby, avoid procrastination.**

### Breaking Down the Task

One commonly used procedure we have found useful is breaking tasks into small, easily completable steps. For example, if you have 40 papers to read—a daunting number—you resist getting started for obvious reasons: The end is very far from the present. If you break the task into ten individual steps, each step involves reading only four papers. These steps, then, could be considered ten small tasks that you can schedule for several days, and they may seem less formidable. If you check off each task as you complete it, you will experience a sense of accomplishment in completing all ten tasks.

While this example involves multiple repetitive tasks, breaking down the task is also useful in dealing with complex, multifaceted tasks. For example, suppose you are assigned the task of creating a curriculum for a new program your school wants to put into place. Such a project may involve a variety of sub-tasks, such as doing research on similar programs currently in use in other institutions, gathering information on your own students that may be relevant to planning the new program, creating appropri-

---

** A fourth strategy, using internal communication to resolve internal conflicts that keep us from completing tasks, is presented in Chapter 10.

ate committees, scheduling planning sessions, creating a working draft, collecting feedback, creating a final draft, and submitting it for approval. Approaching such a large project in its entirety can be overwhelming, but considering each step as a sub-task of the goal to be completed makes the task seem manageable. Another example is being asked to create the schedule for classes for the coming year. Such a task involves finding out when classes can be offered, when rooms are available, checking on previous enrollments, deciding how many sections to offer, making certain that required classes are not taught at the same time, making certain that faculty are scheduled and not double scheduled, creating an initial plan, getting feedback, submitting the schedule, and checking to make certain it gets executed properly. Focusing on only one sub-task at a time in these complicated tasks may make it easier to get started.

### Creating Support

Another commonly used technique for dealing with accomplishing less than you planned involves enlisting the support of a friend or colleague in starting and finishing a task. Sometimes a call or brief conversation at the beginning of each day can help. Also, reporting to the enlisted colleague at the end of each day may prove useful, particularly if you use the opportunity to express pride in your accomplishments and receive acknowledgement, counsel, feedback, and encouragement from your colleague.

### Creating Rewards and Penalties

A third commonly used technique, setting up a system of penalties and rewards, can also help you complete important tasks, and these can be negotiated with yourself, a supportive friend or a colleague. For example, you promise yourself that you will do a highly pleasurable activity immediately upon completing an onerous task. Another approach might be to promise to donate $500 to a cause that you don't want to support if you do not do what is necessary to complete the task. A support person may help you go through with your reward/penalty system.

While we have offered a number of specific, practical procedures to help you reduce the number of uncompleted tasks, we do not pretend that we have exhausted the possibilities. Reasons for not completing tasks (i.e., procrastination) are many, and programs for learning to create results are extensive (for example, see DeVore, 2000). Another approach to completing tasks involves investigating the relationship between the task or tasks you are avoiding and disturbing events in your life (Ferrari, Johnson, & McCown, 1995; Ellis and Knaus, 1977; see also *www.carleton.ca/~tpychyl/refer.html* for an extensive bibliography about procrastination). While none of the strategies we are aware of can guarantee that you will finish all of the tasks in your plan, they will help you get through the experience and develop a set of positive feelings about the experiences associated with completing the tasks.

Finally, we want to acknowledge that we are not all alike. For example, some of us work better under pressure and some of us do not. When we talk with students about procrastination (these conversations frequently occur in the context of writing term papers or completing final projects), a comment we frequently hear is, "I work better under pressure." While we have no reason to doubt that this is true for these students, we also wonder whether they have actually had a recent experience of completing an important task well ahead of time and without pressure. We believe that to know for sure that you work better under pressure, you should give yourself the opportunity to experience both strategies (i.e., working under pressure and working ahead of schedule) to determine which strategy works best for you.

## ELIMINATING THE NEED FOR UNNECESSARY REMEMBERING

As educators, our lives are very complex. A system for managing our use of time allows us to put our energy (and our memories) into more important things than remembering where we need to be at what time. When you make a commitment to manage your time, you also make a commitment to use a time management system. Having a time management system means that you have a place where you can always record what you want to say, do, or think about in the future. When you do your planning each day and look at your prioritized daily task list and appointment schedule, you are reminded of what you need to know. You can stop trying to remember these sorts of things and use your brainpower for other more important tasks.

Finally, in addition to containing information about what you plan to do, most time management systems include provisions for recording important addresses, phone numbers, and memos to your self. Electronic systems also provide provisions for linking information of these types to specific tasks or appointments. Moreover, the memo feature can be used to record thoughts or important ideas as they come up for you.

If you use only one time management system and put all of your important information in a single place, you will always know where to find it. The time management course developed by The Franklin Institute (Winwood, 1990) suggests making a habit of writing notes only in your daily planner or designated notebook and not writing notes on slips of paper, the backs of napkins, or scraps of paper torn off the top of your school newspaper. Suppose, for example, that a colleague has told you she would call you about an important matter. She meets you in the hall several days later and says, "I'm sorry that I didn't call you. I lost your number. Let me write your phone number down again." She pulls a scrap of paper out of her backpack, and you notice that it already has your phone number written on it. We don't think this interaction inspires much confidence in the fact that your phone number will be remembered, but it is a very common scenario. The more often your day planner (or whatever kind of materials you use for managing your time) is with you, the more you will use it, and the more relaxed you will likely feel about your daily schedule and having access to important information.

The portion of this chapter that deals with implementation necessarily focused on the details of managing one's life—appointments, ready references, and schedules. However, the details mean nothing without the big picture. Unless one takes time to link the management of time to one's goals and values (i.e., putting the big rocks in the jar first), time management will be nothing more than a system to simply help you get through the day, remember appointments, and keep commitments. It will not help you generate the deep satisfaction that comes from making time to accomplish the tasks that are nearest and dearest to your heart. Finding pleasure, satisfaction, and privilege in your life and in teaching elude you unless you can create and implement a system for yourself that allows you the time to achieve your most important personal and professional goals.

Implementation and evaluation are keys to developing a system that works for you over time. By reflecting on the intelligence of your plan and the process of implementing it, you can develop a system that works well for you and your life. Moreover, when you reflect on the processes of implementing your plan, you get to know yourself better. You get to know more about how your mind works, how your emotions work, and how your life reflects what you value. Even if you do not necessarily make immediate progress in accomplishing your goals, the progress you make in knowing yourself is always valuable.

We are all allotted exactly the same number of hours in each day. We, and not others, determine how we will use this time. If we replace the common complaint, "I don't have enough time" with "I don't have enough time to do the things I choose to do in the way that I currently choose to do them," we will begin to take some responsibility for our situation. Taking charge of our effectiveness, our management of time, and the dispatch with which we carry out our chosen tasks will give us freedom from feeling out of control and overwhelmed.

## NOTES

1. The focus of the kind of reflection we are describing in this book is on the relationship between our internal worlds and outcomes we want to create in our external world. Other approaches to reflection focus primarily on the relationship between desired and achieved instructional outcomes and steps that can be taken to bring the two more in line (see Richards & Lockhart, 1994; Schön, 1983; Taggart & Wilson, 1998).

"When you get older, you can either get senile or become gracious. There's no in-between. You become senile when you think the world short-changed you or everybody wakes up to screw you. You become gracious when you realize that you have something the world needs, and people are happy to see you when you come in the room. Your wrinkles either show that you're nasty, cranky, and senile, or that you're always smiling."

Carlos Santana
*Guitar Player Magazine*
(August 1999, p. 89)

# Chapter 10

## Harmony

**W**hen we first discovered this quote by Carlos Santana, we said to each other, "You know, he's right! Some people seem to live graciously as they get older, while others do not, and the differences in the paths they have chosen seem to be etched in their faces." We are fortunate in that we have had many good role models for living graciously throughout our careers. Most of our colleagues live what Carlos Santana refers to as gracious lives, particularly as they get older. They seem to spend most of their time enjoying experiences of pleasure, satisfaction, and privilege in relationship to their work. However, as would be expected, we have also known some teachers (as well as ourselves from time to time or even for years at a time!) who do not come across as living graciously. Despite the fact that these teachers have often had remarkably successful careers when evaluated by traditional professional standards, they frequently complain that they or their many achievements are not appreciated or understood and that these achievements have often involved extensive struggles both within themselves and with others.[1] Moreover, these teachers frequently express a belief that these experiences are simply the way things are and that they are in no way responsible for their situations.

Much of the material in this book has dealt with ways of living graciously, or to use a term we prefer, living "harmoniously."[2] Living harmoniously means that we routinely experience our external world from the position of pleasure, satisfaction, and privilege. In order to do this, we must have harmony in our internal world. We gain harmony in our internal world by developing a working knowledge of our internal perspectives, values, and goals and use this knowledge to influence events and relationships in the external world. This book has been about how to make the connection between what is going on in the internal world and how to connect it to the external world. In the process of making the internal and external world connections, it becomes clear that what is going on in one's professional and teaching life is intimately connected to one's personal life. Specifically, the chapters on emotional intelligence, communication strategies, and teacher specialties as well as the chapters on goal setting have all been designed to convey the idea that there are ways to increase the harmony in which we live with others (externally) and within ourselves (internally). Yet, even with the considerable attention we have already paid to harmonious living, we believe that by saying a bit more about this topic we can provide teachers with an even greater appreciation for what internal harmony might be and how one might work to achieve it and to find what is at the heart of teaching for you.

We devote this chapter to exploring ways that two additional hypothesized constructs from psychology—internal communication and projection—can be used to develop a framework for organizing our thinking about harmony. We will conclude with several specific uses of this framework in developing a harmonious internal state from which to seek the heart of teaching. While most of these applications are well known and widely advocated for a variety of reasons, we will look at them through the constructs of internal communication and projection to suggest how they might be of immediate personal value to us as teachers.[3]

## INTERNAL COMMUNICATION

In Chapters 4 and 5, we used a transactional analytic framework to suggest ways in which the internal perspectives of the communicator might influence communication outcomes, and we suggested six strategies (acknowledging, buying time, mirroring, rephrasing, reframing, and questioning) for using this framework to inform ways in which we communicate with others. We now turn our focus from communication with others to communication within ourselves. Here again, transactional analysis provides an introduction to the notion of internal communication. In her overview of the structural components of analysis, Steiner (1974, p. 37–38) describes communication that occurs between what she calls ego states (and which we call *perspectives*) and provides an easy-to-relate-to example. She talks about a man (let's call him Charlie) who is at a party. Charlie has a few drinks and suddenly feels swept away by the music. Charlie begins an expansive, child-like dance. For some moments, Charlie's Internal Child perspective is in the executive or controlling position, and he dances freely. However, at some point, Charlie's perspective changes. In his mind, he imagines other people are looking at him, and he begins to feel embarrassed. A thought such as, "You're making a fool of yourself, Charlie" is generated by the Internal Parent perspective. Charlie stops dancing, and the Internal Parent perspective takes control. These internal dialogues can happen between any two perspectives, and internal messages have been observed by a number of different theorists such as Ellis (1962), Freud (1933), and Steiner (1974).

This example of communication between internal perspectives is one that many teachers may be able to recognize from experience. Let's say that a teacher receives a paper from a student and, after reading it, thinks privately to himself or herself, "This is ghastly!" (This thought obviously comes from the teacher's Critical Parent perspective.) The teacher's Supportive Parent perspective uses the information in the message, reframes it, and communicates the reframed message to the student. The reframed message comes from the Supportive Parent perspective: "I'd like you to focus on paragraph unity. Make sure that each paragraph deals with one controlling idea, and state that controlling idea in the first sentence of the paragraph. I'd also like you to focus on. . . ."

Figure 10.1 illustrates the interaction between the components of the internal and external communication. Any one of the internal perspectives has access to information from the other perspectives, but external communication comes from only one perspective at a time and takes on the output characteristics of that perspective.[4]

**Figure 10.1**  Some Components of Internal and External Communication

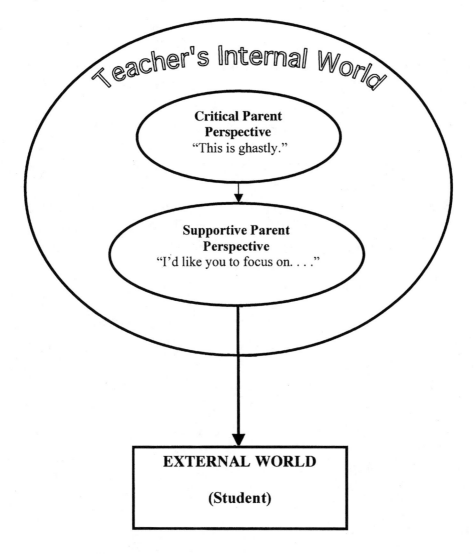

Various psychological disciplines and applications work with internal communication between perspectives, such as Gestalt psychology[*] and Voice Dialog (Stone & Stone, 1989). We will use the term *internal communication* in the general sense to refer to a situation in which one perspective somehow makes its position known to another perspective. Communication in this sense can occur with feelings (as in feeling good about oneself) or with internal pictures (as in mental images of past events or possible future outcomes of actions). For example, in Steiner's example of the self-conscious dancer Charlie, the Parent perspective might interact with the Child perspective. This interaction may not be in words but in terms of a feeling (i.e., the Child perspective in the dancer suddenly feels self-conscious or embarrassed) or in terms of an image in which the Child Perspective "sees" others watching.[**]

In Gestalt psychology, "gestalt" is defined as "a set of elements, such as a person's thoughts and experiences, considered as a whole and regarded as amounting to more than the sum of its parts" *(Encarta World English Dictionary)*. We can use the notion of gestalt defined in this way to establish a link between internal communication and internal harmony. We suggest that internal communication can be thought of as a process by which the internal perspectives can reach an agreement. The agreement itself can be thought of as the gestalt (i.e., the result of interaction among internal perspectives), such that the individual as a whole (as a gestalt) is perceived by others as being in harmony with himself or herself or as "gracious," in Santana's words.

To demonstrate the importance of internal communication to the concept of harmony, we offer the following example of interaction among family members (e.g., parents and children) to illustrate how communication among them might result in either the presence or absence of family harmony. Suppose it is time for a family to plan a vacation. Numerous decisions need to be made, such as where to go, what route to take, what

---

[*]For an extensive, online archive of Gestalt theory and Gestalt psychology see *http://gestalttheory. net/archive*.

[**]In this final chapter, for rhetorical purposes we will often not distinguish between the two Parent perspectives (Critical and Supportive) and the two Child perspectives (Supportive and Adapted) unless doing so is needed to clarify the points being made.

to do for fun, where to eat, when to get up, when to go to bed, and how much to spend. With respect to these decisions, family members might be expected to have different points of view. The children might want to have as much fun as possible. The parents might want to keep everyone physically safe, stay within the budget, and promote various values by focusing on educational or spiritual activities. If the parents summarily impose their point of view on the children and make all of the decisions, the children might not be very happy. The children and the parents will be at odds with each other. Any outsider watching the family closely would observe that the family was not harmonious in their interactions. Conversely, if the parents listen to the children, validate their points of view, and work out a compromise for vacation, the family again becomes more harmonious.

Now consider a similar situation in which the time comes for a single individual to go on a vacation. The same decisions need to be made: where to go, what route to take, what to do for fun, where to eat, when to get up, when to go to bed, and how much to spend. With respect to these decisions, the individual's various internal perspectives might be expected to have different points of view. The Internal Child perspective might want to have as much fun as possible, whereas the Internal Parent perspective might focus on staying safe, keeping to the budget, etc. If the Internal Parent perspective summarily imposes its point of view on the Internal Child perspective and makes all of the decisions, these two internal perspectives will be at odds with each other. Anyone watching this person closely would say he or she was not experiencing harmony. Conversely, if the Parent perspective listens to the Child perspective, validates its point of view, and negotiates with it, the individual might come across to another person as harmonious.[5] Repeated experiences of supportive internal communication contribute to inner harmony (Jeffers, 1992) in the same way that children develop positive self-images through supportive communication with parents (Bean, 1991).

So far, we have considered the idea of internal communication as a possible cause of internal harmony or the lack of it. We now turn our attention to a second hypothesized psychological construct, namely, projection, and consider the role it might play in internal harmony.

## PROJECTION

### *Origins of the Term*

At the core of the theory of projection is "the tendency to make the environment responsible for what originates in the self" (Perls, 1973, p. 35). The commonly used expression, "when you point your index finger at others, your three remaining fingers point back at yourself," illustrates one way that the meaning behind this construct *projection* has found its way into everyday language. Tracing the origins of the term *projection,* von Franz (1980, p. 1) indicates that

> Carl Gustav Jung borrowed the term *projection* from Sigmund Freud, but as a result of his different view of the unconscious, Jung gave that concept a quite separate and new interpretation. He used the word to describe a psychological fact that can be observed everywhere in the everyday life of human beings, namely, that in our ideas about other people and situations we are often liable to make misjudgments that we later have to correct, having acquired better insight.

Projections can be both negative and positive. In non-academic circles, the term projection is generally used to refer to negative misjudgments. However, according to von Franz, "It is...not only a person's negative conscious qualities that are projected outward...but in equal measure his positive ones. The projection of the (positive qualities)...brings about an excessive, delusory, inappropriate overvaluation and admiration of the object" (von Franz, 1980, p. 4).

For example, suppose Teacher A tends to be upset by bossy students or teachers. If Teacher A is told that he himself is bossy and is projecting this judgment on others, Teacher A will tend to deny that his judgment is a projection on the grounds that he is not bossy at all. In the case of positive projection, suppose that Teacher B tends to speak highly of other teachers or students, stating they are highly responsible. If Teacher B is told that she likes others who are highly responsible because she admires that quality so much in herself, she will often tend to reject the projection on the grounds of modesty. The main point here is that when a teacher projects, the teacher does not take full responsibility for his or her own feelings or judgments and finds some way to deny the internal source of the projection.*** We (Palmer & Christison) have certainly experienced our own resistance to taking responsibility for our projections on many occasions, as have many of friends and colleagues who have also waded into the sometimes turbulent waters of the *internal worlds.*

## Source of Projections

Freud hypothesized that both true and false impressions of parents and siblings form the basis of projections (von Franz, 1980, p. 2). For example, if you experience a parent as being bossy, this bossiness may constitute one characteristic of your own Internal Critical Parent perspective. Later in life, you may tend to act bossy whenever your Critical Parent perspective is in charge and, more importantly, to project the characteristic of bossiness on others (to attribute it to others) in the environment who remind you in some way of your Internal Critical Parent.

## Denying Projections

Von Franz also describes the distinction between projection and common error: "The difference between projection and common error is that an error can be corrected, without difficulty, by better information and then dissolve like morning fog in the sunlight. In the case of a projection, on the other hand, the subject doing the projecting defends himself, in most cases strenuously, against correction." (von Franz, 1980, p. 3)[6] Denying projections is a common occurrence. According to Von Franz, "Social workers, educators, and therapists could tell many a tale on this theme; every day they have to struggle with projections, generally those of parental images" (von Franz, 1980, p. 3).[7]

---

***Of course, projections can also be accurate. A teacher may have a "mean-spirited" Internal Critical Parent perspective and may judge others for being mean-spirited when they actually are.

### *Projection as a Process*

Jung uses an interesting metaphor to describe how he sees the process of projection. According to Jung, when we see in others characteristics that remind us in some way of someone we have experienced in the past (usually a parental figure) these characteristics act like "hooks" on which we hang our projected characteristics (von Franz, 1980, p. 3). Here is a hypothetical example from teaching. Let's suppose a teacher had a parent who was older, mean-spirited, and always in charge. This teacher working with a supervisor who shares several hook characteristics such as "older" and "in charge" might project the additional characteristic "mean-spirited" from the teacher's internal world upon the supervisor. The teacher might do this even though the supervisor might not, in the opinions of others, be particularly mean-spirited.[8] Another commonly used metaphor for projections is that of a mirror (MacKeracher, 1996). In this metaphor, the external world serves as a mirror within which an individual doing the projecting "sees" characteristics of himself or herself in the external world.

We represent both of these metaphors (i.e., a hook and mirror) in Figure 10.2. In this figure, "older" and "in charge" are real/shared characteristics (i.e., the hooks) with the characteristics of the environment, in this case, the supervisor. The "mean-spirited" characteristic of the teacher's Internal Critical Parent is projected upon the environment (i.e., the supervisor). The curved, broken arrow from the teacher's internal world to the environment indicates a specific kind of interaction (i.e. projection). This type of interaction is in contrast to the other kinds of interactions described in this book (such as communication strategies, the execution of tasks associated with time management, etc.), which we have represented with straight, unbroken, lines.

Some researchers believe that projected characteristics can become a part of us. Projected characteristics can be thought of as constituting characteristics of the internal world, even if the projected characteristics are vehemently denied. Von Franz states that "if a son, for example, experiences his father as tyrannical, in later life he will, in many cases, not only project the quality of tyranny onto authority figures and father figures, such as his doctor, his superiors, and the state, but he will also behave just

**Figure 10.2**   Hooks and Mirrors as Metaphors for Projection

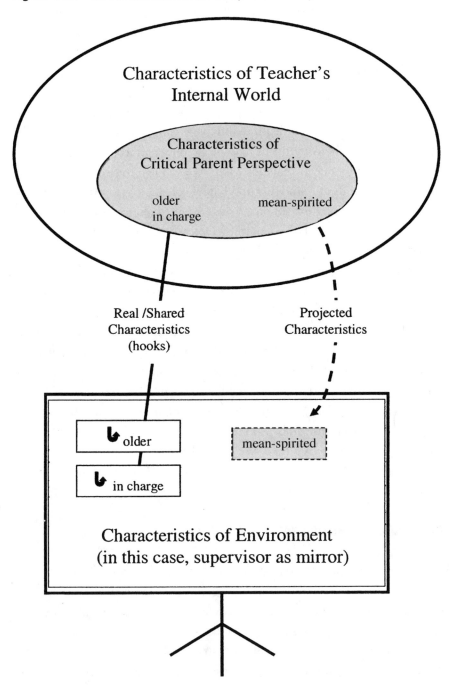

as tyrannically himself—though unconsciously" (von Franz, 1980, p. 3). Moreover, if the son acts tyrannically, his behavior may elicit tyrannical behavior in others.

## SOME APPLICATIONS

Our preceding presentation of the hypothesized psychological constructs of internal communication and projection would not be warranted unless we found them useful in helping us understand possible causes of internal harmony and disharmony and ways to live harmoniously within ourselves and with our students and fellow colleagues. Therefore, we provide five applications for the constructs of internal communication and projection that can make us aware of how we participate in creating our experiences of harmony or disharmony and what we can do to promote the experience of harmony in our lives as teachers. In our point of view, harmony helps lead us to experience teaching as pleasure, satisfaction, and privilege, and ultimately results in our finding what is at the heart of teaching for us.[9] Most of the applications we mention are well known and widely advocated in a variety of circles, including organizational communication (Driskill & Brenton, 2005; Folger, Poole, & Stutman, 2000; Keyton, 2004; Shockley-Zalabak, 2001), and education (Cowan, Palomares, & Schilling, 1992; Mendler, 1992). What may not be so obvious are possible reasons why these applications might work the way they do. We hope that by providing some rationale for their use we will provide incentive to try them out and notice their effects on the experiences of internal and external harmony.

### *Application 1: Resolving Internal Conflict*

Of the five applications that we present, the first one is probably the least commonly practiced. It involves going through a deliberate process of creating an internal dialogue between perspectives. We illustrate this process in the context of a specific example.

One teacher we worked with had struggled for several years to write but found any number of reasons not to do so; she was too tired, she had too many other important tasks, or other things just kept coming up. She eventually found her way into a class designed to help people accomplish goals that they found challenging. In this class, she was given a procedure for allowing her internal perspectives to talk to and eventually negotiate with one another. The teacher reported that one thing she had learned about herself from this class was that one part of her (one internal perspective) clearly wanted to publish the textbook for children, while another part of her did not.[10]

When she became aware of the perspective that wanted to write, her thoughts reflected the following:

*Perspective 1:* "I really want to write. I love to write. I want to make a difference. I have many wonderfully creative ideas."

Another part of the teacher was afraid that she would either fail or become exhausted in the process of writing. When the teacher listened to that perspective, her thoughts changed to the following:

*Perspective 2:* "I'm concerned I will get tired. I won't make any sense. I can't run the risk of getting tired or confused. I won't write."

Once the teacher acknowledged each of the internal perspectives, she interpreted the cause of the problem as the inability of the two perspectives to agree on a course of action. Figure 10.3 represents this problem. The broken arrow between the two internal perspectives represents uncooperative (unharmonious) internal communication. The second broken arrow between the teacher's internal and external world represents a lack of interaction (i.e., procrastination).

The most important feature of this dynamic is lack of agreement between the two perspectives. Using the transactional analysis framework, we would interpret the dynamic as follows: the teacher's Child perspective wants to write, while the teacher's Parent perspective finds reasons why it isn't a good idea.

**Figure 10.3** Internal Communication Leading to Procrastination

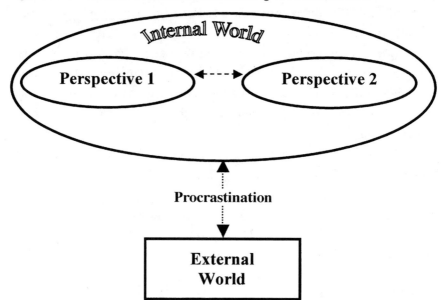

Once the teacher recognized these two internal perspectives and the points of view represented in each one, she was able to start writing. At first, she only wrote for 20 minutes each day because that was what her Parent perspective was telling her. For one week she stopped at exactly 20 minutes, regardless of how well the writing was going or how much or little she had written. Even though 20 minutes was a very short period of time to write, the teacher found the experience rewarding because she was easily able to keep her internal agreement and still make some progress on her writing. After a week, the internal perspective conflict seemed to have been resolved and she decided to increase the number of minutes of writing each day and continued to make progress.

This dynamic is illustrated in Figure 10.4. The solid arrow between the two internal perspectives represents cooperative (harmonious) internal communication. The solid arrow between the teacher's internal and external world represents (inter)action (writing in this case).

While this internal dialogue and the solution to the internal communication problem worked for the teacher in the example, the specific

**Figure 10.4**  Cooperative Internal Communication Leading to Action

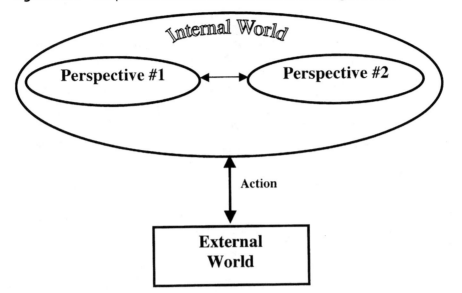

concerns of the two perspectives might be different for other teachers. Moreover, there is no reason to expect that the specific solution agreed on for the teacher in this example would be the solution arrived at for anyone else. However, the process of internal negotiation from a position of internal respect for both perspectives' positions promotes internal harmony in the same way that such a conversation would promote harmony among members of an actual family.[11]

### Application 2:  Taking Responsibility without Shifting Blame or Defending

Taking responsibility is widely advocated as a direct procedure for dealing with a difficult situation while creating as few problems as possible (Branden, 1997). It involves fully acknowledging one's role in contributing to a particular outcome without defending oneself (i.e., offering excuses for one's behavior).[12] The examples that follow illustrate the role internal perspectives play in the ability to refrain from offering excuses for one's behavior.

### Example 1: Taking Responsibility without Shifting Blame or Defending

A teacher has not prepared sufficiently for one of her classes and knows it. A supervisor calls it to the teacher's attention. When one takes responsibility, the thoughts most prominent come from the Internal Supportive Parent perspective.

*Supervisor:* "You haven't prepared sufficiently for your classes."

*Thoughts from the internal Supportive Parent perspective: It's okay to screw up. Everyone does from time to time. Simply admit it to your supervisor.*

*Teacher:* "You're right. I didn't prepare enough. I'll do better next time."

### Example 2: Shifting Blame or Defending

*Supervisor:* "You haven't prepared sufficiently for your classes."

*Thoughts from the Internal Critical Parent perspective: You're lazy, and you shouldn't be. If you admit your mistakes, people will know that you're lazy.*

*Teacher:* "I've been having a lot of troubles at home, and I've been sick a lot.

The process of defending, offering excuses, or shifting blame originates from the Internal Critical Parent perspective. Taking responsibility for one's actions originates from the Internal Supportive Parent perspective.

### *Application 3: Asking for What You Want*

When we are unable to ask for what we want and agree to do something that we don't want, we create disharmony in our internal world.

One internal perspective agrees to something that shows a lack of concern for the views of another internal perspective. These examples illustrate how failure to ask for what one wants might contribute to internal disharmony.

### Example 1: Asking Completely

*Supervisor:* "What courses would you like to teach?"

*Thought from the Internal Child perspective: I want to teach X, Y, and Z.*

*Thoughts from the Internal Supportive Parent perspective: Ask for what you want to teach; you deserve the best.*

*Teacher:* "I want to teach X, Y, and Z."

### Example 2: Holding Back

*Supervisor:* "What courses would you like to teach?"

*Thoughts from the Internal Child perspective: I want to teach X, Y, and Z.*

*Thoughts from the Internal Critical Parent perspective: It's selfish to ask for the class you want. Don't be selfish. You need to think about what other people want to teach.*

*Teacher:* "I'll teach whatever you want me to."

When this teacher holds back, thoughts from the Internal Critical Parent perspective do not consider thoughts from the Internal Child, so the teacher does not ask for what she wants. It is difficult for many people to ask for what they want for a variety of reasons, since an individual's early experiences might impact this process. Uncovering these barriers and working to lower them lie beyond the scope of this book.

### Application 4: Avoiding Harmful Gossip

Avoiding harmful gossip means not engaging in negative communication about a third party who is not present with the intent that the communication does not also acknowledge the projection involved, will be taken seriously, and will be acted upon to punish the third party. We think it goes without saying that the external effects of gossiping about others within an organization are frequently negative. The following example illustrates a possible negative internal consequence of gossiping.

*Colleague:* "Don't you think Attila is mean-spirited?"

*Thoughts from the Internal Child perspective: Sometimes I'm really mean-spirited. I get upset with people and feel that they deserve to be punished.*

*Thoughts from the Internal Supportive Parent perspective: It's normal to feel mean-spirited from time to time.*

*Teacher:* "It's hard to really know, huh? What I do know is that it's possible to feel mean-spirited because I feel that way myself from time to time."

When we accept all characteristics of ourselves rather than judging and excluding them, we can take a more balanced approach to action rather than trying to punish others in the external world. This example illustrates one way to further this process of acceptance. However, in using this example, we do not want to suggest that judgmental gossip is inherently bad or should never be indulged in. In fact, it often seems therapeutic in that it gives direct, uncensored voice to negative thoughts that have a life of their own and can persist for years on end. We only think that it is important to take into consideration the effects of the gossip on others. In some cases, the gossip will be taken only as a whimsical sharing of the individual's internal world but it is not intended to be acted upon. This will likely be the case if we fully own the projection, and we do not see a problem with this in terms of harming others. However, in other cases, gossip is intended to be taken very seriously and is used to poison the working environment. It is up to the individual to decide the intent behind gossip, how it will be taken, and what its consequences are likely to be.

### Application 5: Adopting the Attitude that All Thoughts Are Important

Adopting the attitude that all of our thoughts are important involves noticing our thoughts in their entirety and accepting them. We believe that thoughts originate in the internal perspectives where they wait to make their positions known in the external world. Embracing all of our thoughts is a way of promoting internal harmony without spending too much time trying to figure out from which perspective the thought might be originating.[13] In addition to the strategies described above for accepting one's thoughts, one can also do so by adopting a governing value of acting with kindness in accepting others' behaviors and ideas. Adopting this context for one's life has been widely advocated for millennia in many of the world's spiritual traditions, as shown in this compilation of quotes.[14]

---

**Buddhism**

*Hurt not others in ways that you yourself would find hurtful.*

————Udana-Varga 5,1

**Christianity**

*All things whatsoever ye would that men should do to you, do ye so to them; for this is the law and the prophets.*

————Matthew 7:1

**Confucianism**

*Do not do to others what you would not like yourself. Then there will be no resentment against you, either in the family or in the state.*

————Analects 12:2

**Hinduism**

*This is the sum of duty; do naught onto others what you would not have them do unto you.*

————Mahabharata 5,1517

---

### Islam

*No one of you is a believer until he desires for his brother that which he desires for himself.*

————Sunnah

### Judaism

*What is hateful to you, do not do to your fellowman. This is the entire Law; all the rest is commentary.*[15]

————Talmud, Shabbat 3id

### Taoism

*Regard your neighbor's gain as your gain, and your neighbor's loss as your own loss.*

————Tai Shang Kan Yin P'ien

### Zoroastrianism

*That nature alone is good which refrains from doing another whatsoever is not good for itself.*

————Dadisten-I-dinik, 94,5

When we act with kindness to include others (or at least not to harm them) even if we may have judgments that would exclude them, we give ourselves a positive external experience that may transfer to our internal experience and allow us to include all parts of ourselves. For example, suppose a teacher has negative judgments about a student or colleague and is tempted to act negatively toward that person in some way. If the teacher acts on this judgment, the theory of projection would suggest that she is also acting internally to exclude an unaccepted characteristic of herself. On the other hand, if the teacher acknowledges that her negative judgment begins from within and decides not to act on it, the teacher may well find this non-action actually creates an alternative experience of the student. The teacher might then also realize, if she is honest with herself, that a part of her actually resembles the student she was judging, and the act of treating the student with compassion actually resulted in her feeling more compassion toward herself and, therefore, more internally harmonious.[16]

In considering that all thoughts are important and worthy of being expressed and being heard internally, we are not suggesting that all thoughts should be voiced externally or acted upon. Rather, we are only trying to make the case that within the domain of the individual's internal communication, thoughts originating from the various internal perspectives are important. For example, the Internal Adult perspective needs to be free to assess the facts of different situations, analyze feasibility issues, predict possible consequences of certain behavior, and make plans for the future; and the Internal Parent perspectives need to review governing values, ethical systems, and societal norms.[17] The more we respect our own thoughts as teachers, the more we are likely to respect the thoughts of our students. If we don't reject characteristics of ourselves, we won't reject these same characteristics in others through the process of projection. Our students will feel safer, and we will be able to create more satisfying environments for learning.

## SUMMING UP

*Seeking the Heart of Teaching* is an account of a process we have been involved with for many years. While our account of the process makes use of a number of specific frameworks we have found useful along the way, the fact that we have laid out these frameworks makes no claims about the putative truth of any of them, or of the ultimate nature of the mind, the meaning of life, or ultimate reality. We continue to scrutinize these frameworks that we use to reflect on our own lives, and these frameworks continue to evolve and change.

If we have learned anything from our journey, it is that there are many ways to make sense of our external and internal worlds. Moreover, we are firm advocates of the scientific method in which no hypothesis is ever proven. As a consequence, we continue to feel deep appreciation for the diversity of others' experiences and points of view, as well as the many ways humans have found to live their lives. We look forward to our continued journey, to discovering more about our own processes, and ultimately to learning about and appreciating the processes of others.

> "Now, perhaps you believe that there are no miracles—that each of us lives our destiny—or maybe you chalk it all up to a roll of the dice—that our accomplishments and failures, husbands and wives, our children and the legacy we will leave behind are the result of chance (a tougher, faithless road, unless you can find happiness in embracing blind faith). Yet, everywhere we look, if we are willing to look, there are unmistakable signs of something more complex at work....As the old blues lyric goes, 'I shoulda followed my first mind...Mmm, well if you was suppose to have done that, that's what you would have done did!'"

David Wilson
*ToneQuest Report*
(2003, 4[12], pp. 1–2)

## SUGGESTED READINGS

We would like to recommend three books we have read as much for pleasure as for their educational value. They have served to remind us of the importance of keeping an open mind as we have followed our own individual paths in seeking the heart of teaching and in getting to a place where we experience our lives as teachers predominantly from the experiences of pleasure, satisfaction, and privilege.[18]

*Think: A Compelling Introduction to Philosophy* (Blackburn, 1999)

*The Things We Do: Using the Lessons of Bernard and Darwin to Understand the What, How, and Why of Our Behavior* (Cziko, 2000)

*The Guru Papers: Masks of Authoritarian Power* (Kramer & Alstad, 1993)

## NOTES

1. Richard Nixon and the Dali Lama provide examples of individuals who rose to the position of leadership in their respective countries but had very different experiences of graciousness. The audiotapes of Nixon's private conversations in the White House are often full of bitterness and distrust of a wide range of imagined foes; whereas, accounts of the Dali Lama's life (Campbell, 1988, pp. 158–159) suggest that despite the real persecution that he and the people of Tibet have suffered, he chose not to be bitter and followed instead a path of gracious living.

2. "Harmony" is defined as "a pleasing arrangement of parts" (*The Random House College Dictionary*, 1975, p. 603). For the rest of the chapter we will use this term instead of graciousness because the definition of harmony indicates the interaction of more than one part. In the remainder of this chapter, we will specifically describe what these parts might be in the context of *Seeking the Heart of Teaching* and how they might be pleasingly arranged. It is only a happy coincidence for us that Carlos Santana's quote evoked both musical and existential images of harmony.

3. While we firmly believe that everyone has the right to choose his or her own path through life (within socially agreed-upon norms), we cannot help but feel compassion for those individuals who choose paths that seem to us to be unnecessarily difficult. When such individuals complain about their lot, we can only assume that they would be happier if they had no reason to complain. (We will ignore the secondary gains associated with complaining, such as possible comfort associated with having people with whom to commiserate. For a discussion of secondary gain, see Berne, 1964.) Thus, as much as we have tried to dance around being prescriptive, we do find ourselves promoting harmony as governing value.

4. This is our simplified way of working with the notion of "contaminated ego states" discussed in the transactional analysis literature. For example, Steiner provides an example of a contaminated ego state resulting from an Adult ego state holding as a fact certain ideas stemming from the Parent or the Child (Steiner, 1974, p. 41). We would represent this as the Parent or Child perspective acting through (speaking through) the Adult perspective.

5. Internal harmony can often be observed between what an individual communicates verbally and nonverbally (see Hall, 1973). We associate this congruity with two perspectives in agreement about what is being communicated. We associate a lack of congruity with mixed messages—a lack of agreement among internal perspectives about what is being communicated. For example, if one's Internal Child does something that one's Internal Parent does not approve of, the individual is likely to look uncomfortable or guilty. One part of the individual wants to do something and is doing it, but another part of the individual disapproves of the action.

6. We would note that other theories of projection than those attributed to Jung, Freud, and Perls have been suggested. One such theory is that projection is an essential component of all perception (Hochheimer, 1955). This view of projection is consistent with the encoding of affective schemata along with environment characteristics, but it does not directly address the issue of attributing responsibility. We find it more useful to adopt Jung's position that we could in practice speak of projection only ". . .when the need to dissolve the identity with the object has already arisen," or, in other words, when the identity begins to have a disturbing effect and exerts a negative influence on the adaptation to the outer world (von Franz, 1980, p. 9, quoting Jung [1971, para. 783].) In fact, we find Jung's version of projections most useful in teacher development because we believe that identifying strongly with others often places stress on teachers' abilities to function in a harmonious way.

7. The difficulty in accepting one's judgments as projections is frequently acknowledged in the media. For example, when Jerry Sloan, head coach of the Utah Jazz, was asked whether Utah Jazz forward Andrei Kirilenko was a little stubborn, just like him. Sloan replied, "I don't know that I'm stubborn. I always accuse other people of being stubborn. I don't like to accept myself as being stubborn. But I am stubborn. I don't like to admit that." (Sloan, 2004) It is also often difficult to accept one's judgments as projections when we judge a behavior in others that we *currently* do not engage in. However, we may have engaged in such a behavior in the past, judged the behavior, and decided not to behave that way again. This memory of our past behavior still resides in our minds, and our judgments of this memory can constitute the source of our present-day projection. They remain as part of our internal world.

8. Another possible consequence of projection is that after projecting a certain characteristic (such as bossiness) on the supervisor, a teacher behaves toward the bossy supervisor (that the teacher has created in his mind) in such a way as to elicit bossy behavior on the part of the supervisor. For example, expecting the supervisor to be bossy, the teacher might act in an overtly confrontational way to try to avoid being bossed around and, doing so, provoke the supervisor into bossy behavior as a reaction to avoid being dominated. Or the teacher might act submissively out of fear of the bossiness he projected on the supervisor and, in doing so, evoke an uncharacteristically bossy reaction by the supervisor who might figure that she could easily get away with it. In these ways, our internal experiences and projection might play a role in eliciting external events.

9. A comprehensive approach to pursuing internal and external harmony is a challenge that extends far beyond our limited attempts to try to make sense of it using only two psychological constructs. For example, in the popular literature,

Dyer (2002) presented ten strategies for achieving inner peace, a term we consider synonymous with inner harmony. In the interest of teachability, we limit the extent of our treatment of this topic to two constructs and five applications in order to tie it in as directly as possible to the frameworks developed in the remainder of this book.

10. According to Bandler, Grinder, & Connirea (1989, p. 45), the hypothesis of internal conflict, "that there's a part of you stopping (another part of) you from doing what you want to do," is a fundamental assumption underlying the process of resolving internal conflict.

11. Interpreting decision-making through a framework involving multiple internal perspectives can help us understand why the injunction, "Just do what you want to do" or even, "follow your bliss" (as a way of being happy) can be so difficult to implement. If an individual's internal perspectives are not in agreement about a course of action, the individual will be genuinely ambivalent about what to do, no matter how hard the individual struggles to find a bottom-line answer. Suggesting that an individual act as if this is not true without providing the person with a strategy for resolving the internal discrepancy creates additional pressure without resolving the lack of internal harmony.

12. Providing an excuse along with an apology dilutes the receiver's experience of the wholeheartedness of the apology. In addition, giving an excuse is frequently an indicator of a specialty in overuse. For example, an excuse provided for being late such as, "So and so showed up at the last moment and needed something" might be symptomatic of a specialty in overuse (such as "harassed"). We've said that specialties in overuse can be characterized in different ways and that there is a secondary payoff for the specialty in overuse (such as "Look at how important or caring I am").

13. An extraordinary version of enjoying our thoughts might be construed as an experience of a rapturous feeling of being "one with the universe." Our experience of such states suggests that they are transitory in nature, and attempts to hold onto or recreate them actually result in a lack of inner peace rather than a presence of it. If we set aside extraordinary states of rapture, an ordinary experience that would seem to be available to anyone, regardless of one's spiritual or non-spiritual persuasions or practices, could consist of recognizing that one's experiences are located at least partly in one's thoughts (including thoughts about one's physical and emotional experiences) and then learning to be comfortable with and enjoy these thoughts. For an interesting account of scientific studies of the brain during spiritual experiences using medical imaging technology, see Newberg and Aquili (2001), who reached the conclusion that a large network of different structures in the brain communicate with each other during spiritual or meditative experiences.

This view of spiritual experiences as a chain of objectively observable neurological events seems to be consistent with associating an experience of (internal) harmony with an experience of multiple internal perspectives getting along with one another or communicating in specific ways. These few comments leave unaddressed the nature of the relationship between one's thoughts and whatever the outside world (the universe, in this discussion) might ultimately turn out to be like. This is a question that philosophers have pondered for millennia (see the discussion in Blackburn, 1999, Chapter 7).

14. Adapted from *The Christian Newsletter.* Retrieved February 3, 2005, from http://www.teachingvalues.com/goldenrule.html

15. As we were finishing up this book, a long-time friend of ours, Stephen Krashen, provided us with another version of the principle underlying the Golden Rule that really hit home. We had just come out of a restaurant and seen a homeless person. Perhaps picking up our internal debate over how to respond to the individual, Steve said he had recently been guided by an observation that (in his words), "If you give a beggar the benefit of the doubt, perhaps God will give you the benefit of the doubt." According to Steve, this version of the Golden Rule is based on Irving Bunim's commentary on a passage in *Pirkre Avos* (Hebrew for *Ethics of the Fathers*, see Bunim, 1964.) What struck us about this was the possibility of interpreting it on either literal or psychological levels. Interpreting it literally, we try to improve the chances that an external God will look kindly on our actions. Interpreting it psychologically, we try to improve our chances of creating an internal God-like perspective (a part of our thoughts that we might call "God") that will be gentle with the other parts of ourselves when times get rough.

16. There is no reason why the teacher could not continue to privately enjoy her internal judgments—to take them lightly just as one would take lightly a child's judgments in one's societal family. Irreverent thoughts taken lightly and privately can be quite amusing.

17. The particular treatment of internal harmony we have presented is only one of probably thousands, and voluminous literature on this subject goes back several millennia, all the way to the Rig Veda, which dates from 4000 to 12,000 years BCE, depending on who is doing the dating. A lucid present-day discussion of the nature of the self can be found in Blackburn (1999, p. 263), who describes an intriguing thought experiment designed to demonstrate that the "self" always remains as a perspective. Another recent treatment of the topic can be found in Merzel (2003), who describes a rapid induction technique for giving ordinary people an experience of a non-dualistic mind state as well as ways of making practical use of this experience. Investigating the experience of non-self, Professor Richard Dawkins of Oxford University (2004) found that the induction of a

subject, "Michael," into a spiritual state of self-dissolution was associated with a reduced blood supply to the parietal lobes of the brain, which "typically takes all our sensory information and uses that sensory information to create a sense of one's self."

18. As far as our own thinking goes, we have found that the level of certainty we feel about our ideas is related to the narrowness of our focus. The more we broaden our focus, the more we get in touch with the transitory nature of any particular point of view.

# APPENDIX

## EMOTIONAL INTELLIGENCE QUOTIENT (EQ) INVENTORY
by MaryAnn Christison and Adrian Palmer

**Directions:** Find a quiet place to take your inventory where you will not be interrupted. The statements focus on self-awareness, self-management, self-motivation, and relationship management. Read each statement carefully and thoughtfully. Then honestly rate yourself on each statement on the Likert scale from 1–5 with 1 being the least effective and 5 being the most effective. Remember to reflect carefully on each statement and to be completely honest. There is no point in taking the inventory if you cannot be honest with yourself. Emotional Intelligence begins with self-awareness.

| | Rating Scales | | | | |
| --- | --- | --- | --- | --- | --- |
| | Ineffective | | | Effective | |
| | 1 | 2 | 3 | 4 | 5 |
| 1. I recognize when I am feeling each of the following emotions: anger, sadness, enjoyment, surprise, disgust, shame, and love. | | | | | |
| 2. I keep my promises to others. | | | | | |
| 3. I bring up ethical concerns in my communications with others even if I think it will make the communication somewhat uncomfortable. | | | | | |
| 4. I can publicly admit my mistakes without making excuses. | | | | | |
| 5. I frequently set goals in my life and work to achieve them. | | | | | |
| 6. I am open to new ideas. | | | | | |
| 7. I find it easy to get involved with new people and in new projects. | | | | | |
| 8. I adapt easily to new situations. | | | | | |
| 9. I am even-tempered when unexpected demands are placed on me. | | | | | |
| 10. I have strategies for helping me adapt to new situations. | | | | | |
| 11. I respond positively to opportunities. | | | | | |

| | Rating Scales | | | | |
| --- | --- | --- | --- | --- | --- |
| | Ineffective | | | Effective | |
| | 1 | 2 | 3 | 4 | 5 |
| 12. I initiate communication with others. | | | | | |
| 13. I seek out information and opportunities in my work and personal life. | | | | | |
| 14, I make an extra effort in whatever I do. | | | | | |
| 15. I focus on other people. | | | | | |
| 16. I don't feel compelled to talk about my achievements or myself. | | | | | |
| 17. I listen to others without feeling the need to talk or interrupt. | | | | | |
| 18. I am aware of non-verbal cues in others. | | | | | |
| 19. I respond to non-verbal cues in others. | | | | | |
| 20. I can see others' perspectives. | | | | | |
| 21. I am good at engaging an audience. | | | | | |
| 22. I anticipate the impact of an action or a statement on others. | | | | | |
| 23. I can indirectly influence others. | | | | | |
| 24. I can develop support for ideas and causes. | | | | | |
| 25. I find it easy to get along with and cooperate with others. | | | | | |
| 26. I am effective at soliciting input. | | | | | |
| 27. I encourage others. | | | | | |
| 28. I am good at building bonds with others. | | | | | |
| 29. I can make sacrifices in the short term to achieve long-term goals. | | | | | |
| 30. I reflect on my behavior and my interactions with others. | | | | | |

## SCORING

There are two different ways of working with your score on the EQ Inventory. Calculate your global score. Total your points for the entire inventory. A score between 120–150 means that you have effectively developed your EQ. However, even though your overall score would indicate that you have a well-developed EQ, you should also look carefully at any statements on which you scored below a 2 and determine how you might raise your score on these items. A score of 90–119 means that your EQ is less developed and that you could benefit from changing some behaviors related to these statements in order to raise your overall score. You might do this by targeting one or two items a week on which to focus. A score of 30–89 means that you need concentrated attention on developing your EQ if you want to be successful in your work and in your relationships with others. Target the statements on which you received the lowest score and develop a plan for raising your score to at least 90!

# REFERENCES

Adler R., & Towne, N. (1975). *Looking out, looking in*. Corte Madera, CA: Rinehart Press.

Andreas, S. (1999). *Virginia Satir: The power of her magic*. Moab, UT: Real People Press.

Anthony, E. M. (1963). Approach, method, technique. *English Language Teaching, 17*, 63–67.

Assagioli, R. A. (1972). *Psychosynthesis. A manual of principles and techniques*. New York: Hobbs-Dorman.

Axline, V. M. (1969). *Play therapy*. New York: Ballantine Books.

Bachman, L. F., & Palmer, A. S. (1996). *Language testing in practice: Designing and developing useful language tests*. London: Oxford University Press.

Baker, E., & Holden, J. (1976). An investigation of transactional analysis postulates involving the Parent, Adult, and Child ego state model. In G. M. Goldhaber & M. B. Goldhaber (Eds.), *Transactional analysis: Principles and applications* (pp. 91–111). Boston: Allyn and Bacon.

Bandler, R., & Grinder, J. (1979). *Frogs into princes: Neuro linguistic programming*. Moab, UT: Real People Press.

———. (1982). *Reframing the creative dimensions*. Moab, UT: Real People Press.

Bandler, R., Grinder, J., & Connirea, A. (1989). *Reframing: Neuro-linguistic programming and the transformation of meaning*. Moab, UT: Real People Press.

Barinaga, M. (1992). How scary things get that way. *Science, 258*, 887–888.

Barker, L. L. (1971). *Listening behavior*. Englewood Cliffs, NJ: Prentice-Hall.

Bateson, G. (1972). *Steps to an ecology of mind*. New York: Ballantine Books.

Beahrs, J. O. (1982). *Unity and multiplicity: Multilevel consciousness of self in hypnosis, psychiatric disorder and mental health*. New York: Brunner/Mazel.

Bean, R. (1991). *Four conditions of self-esteem*. Santa Cruz, CA: ETR Publications.

Berne, E. (1953). Concerning the nature of communication. *Psychiatric Quarterly, 27,* 185–198.

———. (1961). *Transactional analysis in psychotherapy*. New York: Grove Press.

———. (1964). *Games people play: The psychology of human relationships*. New York: Ballantine Books.

Blackburn, S. (1999). *Think: A compelling introduction to philosophy*. Oxford: Oxford University Press.

Bloom, B. (1956). *Taxonomy of educational objectives, handbook 1: Cognitive domain.* New York: McKay.

Branden, N. (1997). *Taking responsibility: Self-reliance and the accountable life.* New York: Fireside/Simon and Schuster.

Broadbent, W. W. (1976). *How to be loved.* New York: Warner Books.

Brown, J. D. (1988). *Understanding research in second language learning.* Cambridge: Cambridge University Press.

Brown, N. (2001). *Children of the self-absorbed.* Oakland, CA: New Harbinger Publications.

Bunim, I. M. (1964). *Ethics from Sinai.* Jerusalem: Feldheim.

Cahill, L., Prins, B., Weber, M., & McGaugh, J. L. (1994). Beta-adrenergic activation and memory for emotional events. *Nature, 371,* 702–704.

Campbell, J. (1964). *Occidental mythology: The masks of god* (Vol. III). New York: Viking Penguin.

———. (1988) *The power of myth (with Bill Moyers).* New York: Doubleday.

———. (1990). *Transformations of myth through time.* New York: Harper Perennial.

———. (1992). *The power of myth (with Bill Moyers).* New York: Mystic Fire Video.

Candland, D. (1977). The persistent problems of emotion. In D. K. Candland, J. P. Fell, E. Keen, A. I. Leshner, R. Plutchik, & R. M. Tarpy (Eds.), *Emotion* (pp. 1–84). Belmont, CA: Wadsworth.

Carmichael, C. (2003). *The ultimate ride.* New York: Putnam.

Carnegie, D. (1981). *How to win friends and influence people.* New York: Simon & Schuster Adult Publishing Group.

Carroll, J. B. (1993). *Human cognitive abilities: A survey of factor analytic studies.* New York: Cambridge University Press.

Carver, C., & Scheier, M. (2000). *Perspectives on personality.* New York: Allyn & Bacon.

Chamot, A., & O'Malley, M. J. (1987). The cognitive academic language learning approach. *TESOL Quarterly, 21,* 222–247.

*The Christian Newsletter.* Retrieved February 3, 2005, from http://www.teachingvalues.com/goldenrule.html

Christison, M. A. (1997). Emotional intelligence and second language teaching. *TESOL Matters, 7*(3), 3.

———. (2006). *Multiple intelligences and language learning.* Burlingame, CA: Alta Book Center Publishers.

Clarke, M. A. (2003). *A place to stand: Essays for educators in troubled times.* Ann Arbor: University of Michigan Press.

Covey, S. R. (1990). *The 7 habits of highly effective people*. New York: Simon & Schuster, Fireside.

Cowan, D., Palomares, S., & Schilling, D. (1992). *Teaching the skills of conflict resolution: Activities and strategies for counselors and teachers*. Spring Valley, CA: Innerchoice Publishing.

Critzer, D. (2001, Winter). Visualize the positive behaviors. *The Positive Parenting Newsletter, 3*(2). Retrieved June 20, 2005, from http://www.positiveparenting.com/newsletter/

Csikszentmihalyi, M. (1990). *Flow: The psychology of optimal experience*. New York: Harper & Row.

———. (1996). *Creativity: Flow and the psychology of discovery and invention*. New York: HarperCollins.

———. (1997). *Finding flow: The psychology of engagement with everyday life*. New York: Basic Books.

Cziko, G. (1996). *Without miracles: Universal selection theory and the second Darwinian revolution*. Cambridge, MA: MIT Press.

——— (2000). *The things we do: Using the lessons of Bernard and Darwin to understand the what, how, and why of our behavior*. Cambridge, MA: MIT Press.

Dawkins, M. (2004, February 3). *Secret, strange, and true*. Direct TV, Channel 354, Tech TV.

Descartes, R. (1970). *The philosophical works of Descartes* (Vol. 1) (E. S. Haldance & G. R. T. Ross, Trans.). New York: Cambridge University Press. (Original work published in 1637).

Devore, S. (2000). *The neurophysiology of self-discipline*. Retrieved February 3, 2005, from the SyberVision website: http://www.sybervision.com/Discipline/

Dobbs, T. (2002, April). Mr. Valco. *ToneQuest Report, 3*(6), 10.

Driskill, G., & Brenton, A. L. ( 2005). *Organizational culture in action*. Thousand Oaks, CA: Sage Publications.

Dulay, H., & Burt, M. (1977). Remarks on creativity in language acquisition. In M. Burt, H. Dulay, & M. Finnochiaro (Eds.), *Viewpoints on English as a second language* (pp. 95–126). New York: Regents.

Dyak, M., & Perot, M. (1999). *The voice dialogue facilitator's handbook: A step by step guide to working with the aware ego*. Seattle, WA: L.I.F.E. Energy Press.

Dyer, W. W. (2002). *10 secrets for success and inner peace*. London: Hay House.

Edge, J. (2002). *Continuing cooperative development: A discourse framework of individuals as colleagues*. Ann Arbor: University of Michigan Press.

Ehrman, M. (2000, March 17). *Motivation and defensive style.* Paper presented at the Colloquium on Classroom Applications of Motivation Research, TESOL 2000 Annual Convention, Vancouver, British Columbia.

Ekman, P. (1999). Basic emotions. In T. Dalgleish & M. Power (Eds.), *Handbook of cognition and emotion.* Sussex, U.K: Wiley.

————. (2003). *Emotions revealed.* New York: Times Books.

Ekman, P., & Davidson, R. (1990). *Fundamental questions about emotions.* New York: Oxford University Press.

Elias, M. J., Zins, J. E., Weissberg, R. P., Frey, K. S., Greenberg, M. T., Haynes, N., M., Kessler, R., Schaub-Stone, M. E., & Shriver, T. P. (1997). *Promoting social and emotional learning guidelines for educators.* Alexandria, VA: ASCD.

Ellis, A. (1962). *Reason and emotion in psychotherapy.* New York: Lyle Stuart.

Ellis, A., & Knaus, W. (1977). *Overcoming procrastination.* New York: Institute for Rational Living.

Ernst, K. (1972). *Games students play.* Millbrae, CA: Celestial Arts.

Fagen, J., & Shepherd, I. (1970). *Gestalt therapy now: Theory, techniques, applications.* New York: Harper & Row.

Fairhurst, A., & Fairhurst, L. (1995). *Effective teaching, effective learning: Making the personality connection in your classroom.* San Francisco: Consulting Psychologists Press.

Ferrari, J. R., Johnson, J. L., & McCown, W. G. (1995). *Procrastination and task avoidance: Theory, research, and treatment.* New York: Plenum Publishers.

Fisher, R., Ury, W., & Patton, B. (1991). *Getting to yes: Negotiating agreement without giving in.* New York: Penguin USA.

Folger, J., Poole, M., & Stutman, R. (2000). *Working through conflict: Strategies for relationships, groups, and organizations* (4th ed.). Englewood Cliffs, NJ: Addison-Wesley.

Freud, S. (1933). *New introductory lectures on psychoanalysis.* New York: Norton.

————. (1962). *The ego and the id.* New York: Norton. (Original work published in 1923).

Friedman, H. S., & Schustack, M. W. (2002). *Personality: Classic theories and modern research* (2nd ed.). Needham Heights, MA: Allyn and Bacon.

Gardner, H. (1983). Introduction. In *Frames of mind.* New York: Basic Books.

————. (1993). *Multiple intelligences: From theory to practice.* New York: Basic Books.

Goldhaber, G. M., & Goldhaber, M. B. (1976). *Transactional analysis: Principles and applications.* Boston: Allyn and Bacon.

Goleman, D. (1995). *Emotional intelligence.* New York: Bantam.

———. (1998). *Working with emotional intelligence.* New York: Bantam.

Hall, E. (1973). *The silent language.* New York: Anchor Press/Doubleday.

Hathaway, S., & McKinley, J. C. (2003). *MMPI-2™* (Minnesota Multi-phasic Personality Inventory-2™). Minneapolis, MN: University of Minnesota, Test Division.

Hayley, J. (1993). *Uncommon therapy: The psychiatric techniques of Milton H. Erickson, M.D.* New York: W. W. Norton.

Hendrix, H. (1992) *Getting the love you want: A guide for couples.* New York: Harper-Trade.

Hill, N. (1987). *Think and grow rich.* New York: Random House.

Hochheimer, W. (1955, May). *Über projektion. Psyche,* 283–306.

Horgan, J. (1996, December). Why Freud isn't dead. *Scientific American,* 106–111.

Howe, R. L. (1963). *The miracle of dialogue.* New York: Seabury.

Hunt, D. (1984). *Teaching with a purpose: Instructor's guide and resource book for writing with a purpose by J. M. McCrimmon.* (8ᵗʰ ed.). Boston: Houghton Mifflin.

Hymes, D. H. (1974). *Foundations in sociolinguistics: An ethnographic approach.* Philadelphia: University of Pennsylvania Press.

Janet, P. (1907). *The major symptoms of hysteria.* New York: Macmillan.

Jeffers, S. (1992). *Inner talk for peace of mind.* London: Hay House.

Jensen, E. (1998). *Teaching with the brain in mind.* Alexandria, VA: ASCD.

Jersild, A. (1955). *When teachers face themselves.* New York: Teachers College Press.

Jung, C. G. (1964). *Man and his symbols.* New York: Doubleday.

———. (1971). *The collected works of C. G. Jung. Vol. 6: Psychological types* (H. Read, M. Fordham, G. Adler, & W. McGuire, Eds.). Princeton, N.J: Bollingen Series.

Katie, B. (2000). *All war belongs on paper.* Manhattan Beach, CA: Byron Katie.

Keys, K. (1975). *Handbook to higher consciousness.* St. Mary, KY: Living Love Publications.

Keyton, J. (2004). *Communication and organizational culture.* Thousand Oaks, CA: Sage Publications.

Kornfeld, J. (1994, December). Spiritual maturity. *Unity Magazine,* 65–78.

Kramer, J., & Alstad, D. (1993). *The guru papers: Masks of authoritarian power.* Berkeley, CA: Frog, Ltd.

Krashen, S. (1981). *Second language acquisition and second language learning.* New York: Pergamon Press.

Lakoff, G. (2004). *Don't think of an elephant.* White River Junction, VT: Chelsea Green.

LeDoux, J. (1986). Sensory systems and emotion. *Integrative Psychiatry, 4,* 237–248.

———. (1991). Emotion and the limbic system concept. *Concepts in Neuroscience, 2,* 169–199.

———. (1993). Emotional memory systems in the brain. *Behavioral and Brain Research, 58.*

———. (1994). Emotion, memory, and the brain. *Scientific American, 270*(6), 50.

Levenson, R. W., Ekman, P., & Friesen, W. V. (1990). Voluntary facial action generates emotion-specific autonomous nervous system activity. *Psychophysiology, 27,* 363–384.

Leventhal, H. (1984). A perpetual-mother theory of emotions. In L. Berkowitz (Ed.), *Advances in experimental social psychology, 13* (pp. 139–207). New York: Academic Press.

Mackenzie, A. (1997). *The time trap: The classic book on time management.* New York: American Management Association.

MacKeracher, D. (1996). *Making sense of adult learning.* Toronto: Culture Concepts, Inc.

Maclean, P. (1990). *The triune brain in education.* New York: Plenum Press.

Massimini F., & Carli, M. (1988). The systematic assessment of flow in daily experience. In M. Csikszentmihalyi & I. S. Csikszentmihalyi (Eds.), *Optimal experience: Psychological studies of flow in consciousness* (pp. 266–287). New York: Cambridge University Press.

McKay, M., Davis, M., & Fanning, P. (1981). *Thoughts & feelings: The art of cognitive stress intervention.* Oakland, CA: New Harbinger Press.

McCrimmon, J. M. (1984). *Writing with a purpose* (8th ed.). Boston: Houghton Mifflin.

Mendelsohn, D. (1998). Januz Korzczak: Untunnelling our vision. Lessons from a great educator. In D. Mendelsohn (Ed.), *Expanding our vision: Lessons for the language educator* (pp. 173–186). Ontario, CA: Oxford University Press.

Mendler, A. 1992. *How to achieve discipline with dignity in the classroom.* Bloomington, IN: National Educational Service.

Merton, T. (1998). *The seven storey mountain.* New York: Harcourt/Harvest Books.

Merzel, D. (2003). *The path of the human being: Zen teachings on the bodhisattva way.* Berkeley, CA: Shambhala Publications.

Millon, T. (2006). MIPS® revised (Millon™ index of personality styles revised). Retrieved November 20, 2006, from http://www.pearsonassessments.com/tests.mips.htm

Nagel, M. (2000). *Markers on the path to personal authenticity.* Retrieved June 20, 2005, from http://www.whole-person-counseling.com/Authenticity

Newberg, A., & Aquili, E. (2001). *Why god won't go away: Brain science and the biology of belief.* New York: Ballantine.

Nichols, R., & Stevens, L. A. (1957). *Are you listening?* New York: McGraw-Hill.

Palmer, A. (1998). Joseph Campbell: An inspiration and role model for language teachers. In D. Mendelsohn (Ed.), *Expanding our vision: Lessons for the language educator* (pp. 5–16). Ontario, CA: Oxford University Press.

Peale, N. (1956). *The power of positive thinking.* New York: Random House.

Penfield, W. (1975). *The mystery of the mind.* Princeton, NJ: Princeton University Press.

Peng, C., Yeng. J., & Mueller, D. J. (2003). Construct validity. *Sage encyclopedia of social science research methods* (pp. 181–182). Thousand Oaks, CA: Sage Publications.

Perls, F. (1973). *The gestalt approach and eye witness to therapy.* New York: Bantam Books.

Richards, J., & Lockhart, C. (1994). *Reflective teaching in second language classrooms.* New York: Cambridge University Press.

Richins, M. L. (1997). Measuring emotions in the consumption experience. *Journal of Consumer Research, 24,* 127–146.

Richo, D. (1991). *How to be an adult: A handbook for psychological and spiritual integration.* Mahwah: NJ: Paulist Press.

Robbins, T. (2004, November 3). Interview on *The Edge,* KUTV, Salt Lake City, UT.

———. (1986). *Ultimate power.* New York: Simon and Schuster.

Roberts, A. L. (1975). *Transactional analysis approach to counseling.* Boston: Houghton Mifflin.

Rogers, C. R. (1961). *On becoming a person.* Boston: Houghton-Mifflin.

Sachs, J. (2002). *Aristotle's Nicomachean ethics* (Trans). Newbury Port, MA: Focus Publishing.

Salovey, P., & Mayer, J. (1990). Emotional intelligence. *Imagination, Cognition, and Personality, 9,* 185–211.

Santana, C. (1999, August). Quest for fire. *Guitar Player Magazine,* 89.

Schön, D. (1983). *The reflective practitioner: How professionals think in action.* New York: Basic Books.

Schumann, J. (1997). *The neurobiology of affect in language.* Malden, MA: Blackwell.

Schwartz, R.C. (1995). *Internal family systems therapy.* New York: The Guilford Press.

Shalaway, L. (1989). *Learning to teach.* New York: Scholastic Books.

Shapiro, D. (1965). *Neurotic styles.* New York: Basic Books.

———. (1989). *Psychotherapy of neurotic character.* New York: Basic Books.

———. (2000). *Dynamics of character: Self-regulation in psychopathology.* New York: Basic Books.

Shepherd, P. (2007). Transforming the mind. Retrieved January 21, 2007, from http://www.trans4mind.com/transformation/transform.3.17.htm

Shockley, Z. P. (2001). *Fundamentals of organizational communication: Knowledge, sensitivity, and values.* Needham Heights, MA: Allyn & Bacon.

Sloan, J. (2004, February 8). Interview on *Sports Beat Sunday*, KSL TV, Salt Lake City, UT.

Solms, M. (2004, May). Freud returns. *Scientific American,* 82–88.

Sprinthall, N. A., & Sprinthall, R. C. (1990). *Educational psychology: A developmental approach* (5th ed.). New York: McGraw-Hill.

Steiner, C. (1974). *Scripts people live: Transactional analysis of life scripts.* New York: Grove Press.

Sternberg, R. J. (1985). *Beyond IQ: A triarchic theory of human intelligence.* New York: Cambridge University Press.

———. (1988). *The triarchic mind: A new theory of human intelligence.* New York: Cambridge University Press.

Stevick, E. W. (1976). *Memory, meaning & method: Some psychological perspectives on language learning.* Rowley, MA: Newbury House.

———. (1980). *Teaching languages: A way and ways.* Rowley, MA: Newbury House.

———. (1982). *Teaching and learning languages.* New York: Cambridge University Press.

Stone, W. (1962). *The success system that never fails.* Englewood Cliffs, NJ: Prentice-Hall.

Stone, H., & Stone, S. (1989). *Embracing ourselves.* Mill Valley, CA: Nataraj Publishing.

Taggart, G., & Wilson, A. (1998). *Promoting reflective thinking in teachers: 44 action strategies.* Thousand Oaks, CA: Corwin Press.

Trungpa, C. (1973). *Cutting through spiritual materialism.* Berkeley, CA: Shambhala Press.

Vitz, P. (2005). The psychology of atheism. Retrieved January 29, 2005, from the John Mark Ministries website: http://jmm.aaa.net.au/articles/8968.htm

von Franz, M. L. (1980). *Projection and re-collection in Jungian Psychology.* London: Open Court.

Wardhaugh, R. (2002). *An Introduction to sociolinguistics* (4th ed.). Malden, MA: Blackwell.

Watkins, J. G., & Johnson, R. J. (1982). *We, the divided self.* New York: Irvington.

Watzlawick, P. (1978). *The language of change.* New York: Basic Books.

Wertsch, J. (1985). *Culture, communication, and cognition: Vygotskian perspectives.* Cambridge: Cambridge University Press.

Westberg, J., & Hilliard J. (1994). *Teaching creatively with video: Fostering reflection, communication, and other clinical skills,* New York: Springer Publishing.

White, T. (1980). Freud and Berne: Theoretical models of personality. *Australasian Journal of Transactional Analysis, 2,* 1.

Wilson, D. (2003). *The ToneQuest Report, 4(12).*

Winwood, R. (1990). *Time management: An introduction to the Franklin system.* Salt Lake City, UT: Franklin International Institute, Inc.

Woods, T. (2001, October 10). Interview on *The Oprah Winfrey Show,* ABC Television.

# SUBJECT INDEX

# AUTHOR INDEX